Hitler's Sky Warriors

German Paratroopers in Action 1939–1945

Hitler's
Sky Warriors

German Paratroopers in Action 1939–1945

Christopher Ailsby

SPELLMOUNT

Staplehurst

British Library Cataloguing in Publication Data:
A catalogue record for this book is available
from the British Library

Copyright © 2001 Brown Partworks Limited

ISBN 1-86227-109-7

First published in the UK in 2001 by
Spellmount Limited
The Old Rectory
Staplehurst
Kent TN12 OAZ

3 5 7 9 8 6 4 2

Editorial and design:
Brown Partworks Ltd
8 Chapel Place
Rivington Street
London
EC2A 3DQ
UK

Editor: Peter Darman
Picture research: Christopher Ailsby
Design: Brown Partworks

Printed in Hong Kong

Picture Credits
All photographs Christopher Ailsby Historical Archives except:
The Robert Hunt Picture Library: 2-3, 8, 14, 20, 38 (both), 39, 42 (both),
43, 44 (top), 45 (bottom), 46, 49, 50 (both), 52, 53 (both), 54 (top), 55 (both),
57, 58, 59, 60, 62, 83, 84, 85 (bottom), 88 (bottom), 89 (top), 92, 96 (bottom),
97, 98, 100 (both), 102, 103 (bottom), 106, 110, 111 (both), 112 (bottom),
115 (bottom), 116 (bottom), 117, 132, 142, 143 (both), 146, 149, 151 (top),
155, 157, 158, 159, 160, 164, 165, 166, 167, 169, 170, back cover

Pages 2–3: Victorious Fallschirmjäger on the Gran Sasso plateau following the
rescue of Mussolini, September 1943.

CONTENTS

Above: *The top hatch gunner of a DFS 230 glider photographed during a training exercise. His rank is Gefreiter (Lance-Corporal), as indicated by his collar patch and single arm chevron.*

ORIGINS OF THE FALLSCHIRMJÄGER

Though Germany only started to become interested in the raising of airborne forces in the mid-1930s, under the auspices of the Nazis the foundations were established upon which an entire airborne division could be created. But first an air force and air industry had to be created from scratch following defeat in World War I.

Left: *A Fallschirm-jäger battalion on parade during World War II. Note Luftwaffe eagles on the smocks. The two men on the left are officers – they are wearing Luftwaffe officers' belts, with open two-pronged buckles. The others wear standard-issue alloy buckles, as issued to other ranks.*

The development of the German Fallschirmjäger (parachutists) formations can be traced back to the years preceding World War I. During the years between 1900 and 1914, two major revolutionary military developments emerged. The first was the submersible; the second, and more junior, was powered flight. All Europe was fascinated by the latter, being beguiled by the fantasies and hysteria that surrounded it. In Germany in particular there was much interest shown in powered flight, although in Great Britain the relevant authorities were sceptical. In 1909, for example, the British Committee of Imperial Defence reported that "it had yet to be shown whether aeroplanes are sufficiently reliable to be used under unfavourable weather conditions. The committee has been unable to obtain any trustworthy evidence to show whether any great improvement was to be expected in the immediate future". The high cost of an aeroplane, £1000, was noted and the committee concluded that £45,000 should be invested in airship research instead. The War Office

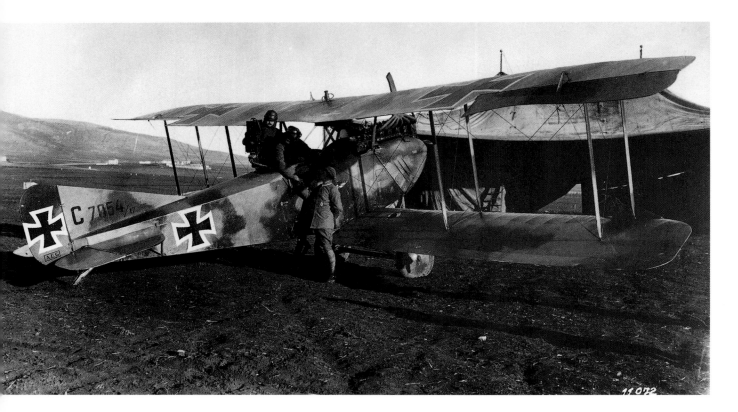

soon announced that aeroplane experiments had ceased "as the cost has proved too great: £2500". Meanwhile, by 1909 the French had expended the equivalent of £47,000 on aeroplanes for the army. The Germans, wishing to dominate the fledgling science, spent the equivalent of £400,000 on aeroplane research alone.

In Germany an aviation test project was set up, overseen by Captain de le Roi of the German War Ministry, and a technical section was established under a staff officer, Major Hesse. To link the efforts of the army with those of private industry, an inspectorate was established under the command of Lieutenant-General Freiherr von Lyncker. The result of this unification between government and industry was the establishment of an aircraft design agency. In 1909, aircraft were used by the military for the first time during manoeuvres watched by Kaiser Wilhelm II. The following year saw the establishment of the first flying schools, and on 8 July 1910 Captain de le Roi assumed command of the provisional flying school at Döberitz. The Flying Command Döberitz consisted of Captain de le Roi, together with Lieutenant Geerdtz, and Second Lieutenants Mackenthun and von Tarnoczy. A week later the four began their flying instruction, and by the middle of December the next six officers had completed their course of instruction. The German War Ministry, impressed by the promising results of the flying school, allocated a sum of 110,000 Marks for the purchase of aircraft – the first step towards a German air force had been taken. A system of pilots' licences had also been introduced in 1910, administered by the German Aviation Association and the Inspectorate of Transport for Military Troops and Civilian Pilots. The first to gain one was August Euler on 1 February 1910. To reward military pilots and to give an outward recognition of their prowess, the Kaiser introduced the Military Pilots' Badge on 27 January 1913.

With the outbreak of World War I in August 1914 the importance of aerial warfare was initially overlooked. The general staffs of the combatant nations considered it a toy of dubious use, and those in the infant air services were looked upon as "backsliders" who had found a way of avoiding "real" action.

Above: *German airmen of an AEG CIV prepare for a mission during World War I. During the last few months of the war German pilots were equipped with parachutes. The use of parachutes by pilots was frowned upon by the British Air Board, which stated: "It is the opinion of the Board that the presence of such an apparatus [a parachute] might impair the fighting spirit of pilots and cause them to abandon machines which might otherwise be capable of returning to base for repair." Instead of parachutes, the board advocated armour plating to protect aircraft and their crews.*

Speaking as Commander-in-Chief, Aldershot, just one month before the outbreak of war, for example, Sir Douglas Haig, later commander of the British Expeditionary Force, told a military gathering: "I hope none of you gentlemen is so foolish as to think that aeroplanes will be able to be usefully employed for reconnaissance in the air. There is only one way for a commander to get information by reconnaissance and that is by the use of cavalry."

First faltering steps

The British Royal Flying Corps (RFC) went to war with just 197 pilots. Two weeks later Sefton Brancker, Director General of Military Aeronautics, compiled a list of all those left in the country able to fly, and discovered that only 862 men held the Royal Aero Club's certificate. Of these, just 55 were sufficiently advanced to undertake active service immediately. Such meagre resources were considered no great handicap, however, as each side discounted aerial combat (no aircraft mounted any guns) and thus any losses were expected to be small. By the summer of 1915, there were only 200 pilots undergoing training in Great Britain and so it was assumed that weekend gentlemen aviators would top up the supply. In its wisdom the War Office decreed that "members of the RFC who own their own aeroplanes should be encouraged to bring them to the Central Flying School when they undergo their training". In addition, before RFC acceptance all the candidates had to obtain the necessary Aero Club certificate of competence, and had to pay the £75 fee. Entry qualifications to the RFC were eccentric: individuals were asked if they could ride a horse, a motorcycle or sail a boat. Then, after picking out strands of differently coloured wools, individuals were pronounced medically fit to fly.

During the course of the war the "knights of the air" of the fledgling air forces were to prove their military worth, especially after the introduction of synchronised machine guns, which enabled them to fire through the propellers

Below: *Fallschirmjäger recruits board a Dornier Do 23 bomber for a training jump in the mid-1930s. The Do 23 was one of the first bombers to equip the new Luftwaffe. It was soon discovered that it had many drawbacks, not least being underpowered and beset with handling faults. By 1939 this twin-engined aircraft was obsolete and had been relegated to training duties, such as providing jump platforms for the fledgling airborne arm. Note the external tubular knee pads worn by each jumper. Constructed of leather-covered sponge rubber, they were held in position by a set of two strong elasticated and adjustable straps which crossed behind the knees and clipped onto the button hooks on the opposite side of the pad.*

Left: *The German Army Parachutists' Badge. Before being amalgamated with Luftwaffe units, the army's parachute formation awarded its personnel a parachute qualification badge (shown here). Instituted in June 1937 and awarded up to January 1939, it comprised a gold wreath of oakleaves with the folded-wing Wehrmacht eagle and swastika at the top centre. Within the wreath was the diving eagle with empty talons. The badge was awarded on completion of six parachute jumps, and it was necessary for recipients to make at least six jumps a year to retain the award. Army badges were allowed to be worn on Luftwaffe uniforms by ex-army paratroopers after they had been absorbed into Luftwaffe Fallschirmjäger units.*

Right: *The Glider Pilots' Badge, which was instituted on 16 December 1940. It consists of a wreath of oakleaves made up of eight bunches of three leaves on either side, the edges of the leaves forming the inner and outer edges of the wreath. They meet tip-to-tip at the apex with a swastika at the base. On the wreath is a soaring eagle, flying from left to right, with a well-defined head positioned over the forward-thrusting wing. As the war progressed the quality of the badge deteriorated, not so much in the stamping of the individual wreath and eagle but the way in which the eagle was attached to the wreath and the quality of the metal used. The badge was awarded on completion of glider pilot training and was issued with a citation and pilots' licence. It was usually worn on or a little below the left breast pocket of the flying tunic.*

of their aircraft. Aerial dogfights became common, and a disturbing degree of visibility often accompanied death in the air. On the ground, among thousands of other men in a vortex of deafening noise, a shot infantryman would fall unnoticed, and a few lumps of red meat would be all that remained following a direct hit by an artillery shell. High in the sky, however, encased in canvas and wood, the dying airman seem to amplify his death by falling in slow motion and often in flames, a sight watching pilots never forgot. Later in the war, it was always made worse in the minds of British pilots by the fact that the enemy had a better chance of surviving a jump. They used parachutes of British design, modified only by a cord attached to the fuselage which ripped open the 'chute when needed. Many German pilots survived, such as the aces Ernst Udet (jumped once) and Josef Jacobs (jumped twice). Nevertheless, neither the RFC nor the later Royal Air Force (RAF) were ever issued with parachutes. The fact that they weighed as much as a machine gun might have had some bearing on the matter.

Above: *A Fallschirmjäger unit on parade "somewhere in Germany". From the start the detail of airborne clothing was given great attention. These paratroopers, for example, are wearing black leather gloves as part of their parade uniforms. Of the gauntlet design, they were made of black leather and were elasticated on the back to give a tight fit to the wrist and lower forearm. For summer wear they were not lined, but for winter issue they were lined with fur for warmth.*

Early parachute experiments

In Great Britain it was not until 1935 that serious parachute testing took place under official Air Ministry supervision, although a demonstration jump from an airship, using this design of parachute, had taken place in 1913. In addition, an unauthorised jump from the parapet of Tower Bridge in London, by Major Orde-Lees in 1917, showed that parachutes could open successfully from a height of only 46.6m (153ft).

As well as saving lives, parachutes could be put to a more offensive use. To break the deadlock of the Western Front, Brigadier-General Billy Mitchell, commander of the US Air Corps in France in 1918, proposed that parachute battalions should be raised and dropped behind the German lines at Metz. The Allied High Command concluded that such unique operations would take at least six months to plan, organise and equip. In addition, there were insufficient aircraft to transport the paratroop battalions in a single lift, combined with the problem of the immediate availability of parachutes. The idea was therefore abandoned, and the cessation of hostilities in the West in November 1918 brought the war to an end.

German aviation after World War I

By 1918 aircraft had changed the nature and conduct of war (by the Armistice, the original 197 British pilots had become 26,000), even if conservative elements within military hierarchies chose to believe otherwise. Haig, for example, saw no reason to change his general opinion on the military value of aircraft. In his personal draft for a final despatch, just two sentences were given to the air: "Though aircraft and tanks proved of enormous value, their true value is as ancillaries of infantry, artillery and cavalry." The reason he gave for this poor rating was that "the killing power of the aeroplane is still very limited as compared to the three principal arms". However, the architects of the Treaty of Versailles in June 1919 acknowledged the potential of military aircraft, and

Below: *The former German heavyweight boxing champion Max Schmeling (second from left) was a famous Fallschirmjäger volunteer who fought on the island of Crete. Here he is seen about to board a Junkers Ju 52 for a winter practice jump before World War II. The men are holding the static lines of their parachutes in their left hands. Boarding the aircraft required both hands and so the line would usually be placed in the mouth as individuals hauled themselves aboard. All paratroopers received extensive training in packing their own parachutes, thus making each individual responsible for his own safety.*

its clauses stated that the German Air Force was to be dissolved, its aircraft confiscated or broken up. Furthermore, the production of aircraft and aero engines in Germany was forbidden. However, these measures failed to halt developments in military aviation in Germany.

Sports clubs sprang up all over Germany after the war, which undertook to teach aeronautically minded Germans the art of flying. In addition, the Reichswehr (the 100,000-strong army allowed to the new Weimar Republic by the Treaty of Versailles), fearing that it was being left behind in military developments, secretly negotiated with the Soviet Red Army in early 1923 regarding training facilities. It finally signed an agreement in April 1925 which made Lipezk Airfield in Russia available for German military training. In 1926, besides the fighter pilot training that was already underway there, observer training began. Added to this, a special unit for testing new aircraft, weapons and equipment was also included.

Hitler boosts the aviation arm

Between 1925 and 1933 approximately 120 officers returned from this flying school in Russia, having been fully trained as fighter pilots. Those who returned during this period maintained their skills by being incorporated as civilian

Above: *Hermann Göring, the overweight, flamboyant head of the Luftwaffe who was instrumental in creating Nazi Germany's airborne formations after observing the Red Army parachute displays in the mid-1930s. Though it was Kurt Student who turned the airborne arm into an élite, it was Göring who created the environment in which Student could work to maximum effect. He did this in two ways. First, he organised, trained and built Germany's air arm. Second, he consolidated all the Reich's airborne units within the Luftwaffe.*

Above: *The Junkers Ju 52 was the backbone of the Fallschirmjäger's airlift capacity and is shown here in its civil capacity (where it was a passenger aircraft). Some 4845 of the rugged and reliable "Auntie Jus" or "Iron Annies" were built by Nazi Germany, and they served in a variety of roles: magnetic-mine destroyers, glider tugs, troop transports, freighters and casualty evacuation ambulances. The Ju 52 could carry up to 16 fully equipped paratroopers over a range of 1300km (808 miles) at a speed of 305km/h (190mph).*

pilots flying for the fledgling Lufthansa airline. The airline also employed the best veteran pilots from World War I, and so the two sets of pilots flew together and gained experience from each another.

Adolf Hitler, leader of the National Sozialistische Deutsche Arbeiterpartei (National Socialist German Workers' Party) – NSDAP or Nazi Party – became Chancellor of Germany in January 1933. Within months he had assumed absolute power within Germany, and began a ruthless campaign to transform Germany into a military machine to implement his expansionist policies. In the same year he created the Deutscher Luftsport-Verband (DLV), an organisation designed to stimulate interest in aviation. The club offered its members, most of whom had previously been in the armed forces, the active disciplined life for which they yearned, to such an extent that on 10 November 1933 Hitler granted the DLV its own uniform with rank and trade insignia. Under the direction of this organisation the members learned three main aeronautical skills: ballooning, glider-powered flight and parachuting. In 1933 Hitler also abandoned the school at Lipezk, and thus placed reliance on the DLV to train new personnel for his clandestine Luftwaffe (Air Force).

The Luftwaffe flexes its wings

As the Nazi Party assumed an iron grip over Germany Hitler became more confident on the international stage, and on 26 February 1935 he announced the official formation of the Luftwaffe. All the secrecy that had surrounded it was blown away. The DLV was disbanded and all its former members encouraged to join the new National Sozialistische Flieger Korps (National Socialist

Flying Corps) – NSFK – which was introduced in its place. In this manner the Nazi Party brought together under its control all of the country's flying clubs into one, essentially paramilitary, organisation. The NSFK could thus operate side-by-side with the fledgling Luftwaffe, and both were able to grow and gather strength together.

In April 1935, the first German fighter squadron emerged under the command of Major Ritter von Greim, bearing the title Jagdgeschwader Richthofen 2. The fighters made their first public display during the occupation of the Rhineland (which had been demilitarised under the terms of the Treaty of Versailles) on 7 March 1936. The first Luftwaffe fighter school was established at the Deutsche Verkehrsfliegeschule (German Commercial Pilots' School) at Schlelssheim, thus completing the formation of the new Luftwaffe and the NSFK. Through skilful propaganda and deception it appeared that Hitler had created a force as technically advanced as the Luftwaffe virtually out of thin air. This feat tended to add to Hitler's international diplomatic aura, the more so during the Luftwaffe's involvement in the Spanish Civil War (1936-1939), where its reputation as a "terror machine" was confirmed during such incidents as the bombing of Guernica in April 1937.

Below: *Fallschirmjäger photographed prior to boarding a Ju 52. During the early history of the airborne arm there was a shortage of these three-engined aircraft, so recruits had to make jumps from a variety of aircraft. These included Dornier Do 23s, Heinkel He 111s and Savoia-Marchetti S.M. 81s. The latter was a three-engined Italian bomber that resembled the Ju 52 in appearance. Note parachute harnesses, leather gloves, helmets and knee pads.*

As mentioned previously, the idea of placing a large body of troops inside enemy territory was first mooted during World War I. In the interwar period Germany was a late starter in the development of airborne forces, though far in front of Britain, the United States and Japan. The potential of airborne forces was, perhaps surprisingly, first recognised in Italy and the recently created Soviet Union. The first effective static-line parachute was developed in Italy during the 1920s. Static-line parachuting, whereby parachutes are attached to the inside of an aircraft and are opened automatically when troops leave the aircraft, was essential for massed paratroop operations. Individual rip-cord opening would have required drops from higher altitudes, with the inevitable higher casualties and worse scattering. Training would also have been more complex and dangerous. The Soviet Union demonstrated the military potential of airborne forces in the early 1930s, though its methods were crude. The troops had to leave their slow-moving ANT-6 aircraft through a hole in the fuselage roof, then gingerly edge their way out along the wings, before jumping together and immediately pulling their rip-cords. This was hardly a safe arrangement, though

Below: *Another show of Fallschirmjäger strength before the outbreak of World War II. Despite the fact that the Soviets had first developed the idea of parachuting large numbers of troops behind enemy lines, by the late 1930s it was the Luftwaffe that had perfected military parachuting skills and created a formidable airborne force. From the beginning all recruits to the Fallschirmjäger were volunteers, which resulted in a high level of morale and motivation. These troops are equipped with 7.92mm Gewehr 98s, the standard personal weapon of the German Army.*

Above: *Of interest in this photograph of Fallschirmjäger personnel is the army's straight-winged national emblem worn on the right breast of the officer saluting and leading the marching column. This indicates he is a former member of the army's Fallschirm-Infanterie-Bataillon (Parachute Infantry Battalion), which was absorbed into the Luftwaffe on 1 January 1939, becoming the 2nd Battalion of the 1st Parachute Regiment.*

Left: *These paratroopers are wearing the second-pattern Luftwaffe smock, which was manufactured in pale green or grey cotton. It was a step-in blouse with a central front opening from neck to crotch with a fly-fronted heavy duty brass zipper, although early models had buttons. Each blouse leg had a single press-stud to gather and secure the leg ends (note photographer).*

it did result in a very tight grouping on the drop zone, especially when one considers that the aircraft had to slow to a speed of 96km/h (60mph), not much above stall, in order to make the operation feasible! At such a speed surprise was hardly possible, and the aircraft themselves would have been especially vulnerable to ground fire, even from small arms.

German military thinkers also appreciated the flexibility in attack which airborne forces could provide, and turned their thoughts to what could be accomplished "at home". Perhaps they were thinking of the smiling remark which Red Air Force Marshal Michal Schutscherbakov had made to the French Marshal Pétain during a tour of the Maginot Line defences along the Franco-German border: "Fortresses like this may well be superfluous in the future if your potential adversary parachutes over them." Hermann Göring, head of the Luftwaffe, was among the German observers to the Russian manoeuvres in 1935 and 1936, and had witnessed parachuting onto an objective by a regiment of 1000 troops, followed by the airlandings of transport aircraft carrying reinforcements of another 2500 fully armed men together with their heavy weapons. These two types of airborne soldiers had then carried out conventional infantry attacks covered by fire from machine guns, mortars and light artillery.

Above: *The Luftwaffe Parachutists' Badge. Instituted in November 1936, it comprised a diving eagle in gold clutching a swastika in its talons, surrounded by a laurel wreath. Like its army equivalent, it was awarded on the successful completion of six parachute jumps.*

Parachuting and airlanding

All the invited observers were undeniably impressed. One of the British Army's highly experienced and much-decorated soldiers of World War I, Major-General Archibald Wavell, wrote at the end of those exercises: "If I had not seen it for myself, I should not have believed such a thing to be possible." However, Wavell also expressed reservations as to their tactical value: how would lightly armed, sparsely supplied paratroops hold out against forces deployed to repel them, especially tanks? Nevertheless, the Red Army had demonstrated that conflagrations of the future would have a new dimension. It is axiomatic that in times of war a nation will deploy its land forces to counter perceived threats — along borders, coastlines and the like — and will leave its heartland relatively lightly guarded. The means had been developed to attack an opponent's vulnerable rear areas in strength: height would now be added to those of width and depth (the concept of "vertical envelopment").

At this point a distinction must be drawn between the two main types of airborne soldier. Parachute troops are trained to jump from aircraft, whereas airlanding troops are flown into the drop zone in aircraft and disembark once on the ground. On the eve of World War II, for example, the Luftwaffe possessed the 7th Flieger (Airborne) Division, composed primarily of paratroopers, whereas the army possessed the 22nd Infantry Division, which had been trained and equipped to operate with aircraft. Designated "Airlanding Division", none of its men were parachute trained. Their specialist training consisted of being able to disembark from aircraft on the ground at speed.

Blitzkrieg and the use of airborne forces

By the late 1930s, Germany's armed forces were trained and equipped for the tactical and strategic concept of the Blitzkrieg (Lightning War). This theory of attack was based on the premise that it is simpler, easier and cheaper to destroy an opponent's armed forces by cutting off its supplies or by severing its lines of communications and control than by frontal assaults. Allied to this premise were the elements of speed and shock.

On the ground armoured spearheads, supported by artillery and dive-bombers, would smash through the points of least resistance, fan out, bypass enemy strongpoints, and sweep around road and rail junctions, paralysing enemy supply, reserve and command elements. Follow-on units would capture or encircle defenders as the spearheads plunged deeper into enemy territory towards towns and cities. Surprise and large-scale attacks on the enemy's air force and airfields at the beginning of the campaign would ensure total German air superiority throughout the Blitzkrieg attack. The use of airborne troops to seize key points ahead of the armoured spearheads fitted well into this strategy. They could take and hold key points until the attacking ground forces arrived. During the war German airborne forces also proved that they could capture islands and hold them independently of ground forces. But such airborne missions required special training, equipment and personnel, as well as commanders and junior leaders with vision and drive.

Below: *Kurt Student (right). Born in 1890, he was a pilot in World War I and thereafter took a special interest in parachuting. As the Inspector of Flying Schools he became involved with the parachute training school at Stendal. On 1 July 1938, Generalmajor Student assumed command of the Luftwaffe's airborne forces, and with Major Gerhard Bassenge, commander of the Stendal school, was responsible for the establishment of the 7th Flieger Division (7th Airborne Division). By combining rigorous training with imaginative tactics and good equipment, he made the division an élite formation. Kurt Student died at Lemgo, Germany, on 1 July 1978.*

Above: *A section on parade. Note the bandoliers for 100 rounds of rifle ammunition with press-fastened pockets, and holsters containing Sauer 7.65mm Model 38(H) handguns.*

ORGANISATION AND TRAINING

The growth of the Fallschirmjäger was a rather haphazard affair throughout the 1930s, but the ambitions of the head of the Luftwaffe, Hermann Göring, was to have a beneficial effect on the airborne arm, which meant that by the outbreak of World War II Germany possessed a fully fledged airborne division.

Left: *An Unteroffizier (Sergeant) shows the jump position from a Ju 52. The sequence of orders for a parachute jump was as follows: Get Ready; Hook Up; Get Ready to Jump; GO! Note the static lines exposed at the door, indicating jumpers who have already jumped.*

The development of Germany's airborne forces prior to World War II was haphazard, though by the outbreak of war in September 1939 the Luftwaffe possessed a highly motivated and trained airborne division, albeit understrength.

Less than one month after Hitler's ascension to power in January 1933, Hermann Göring, at the time Prussian Minister of the Interior, ordered the creation of a special police unit which "in complete devotion to the Führer, would be capable and willing to stamp out any spark of resistance before it could become a threat to the young National Socialist movement". On 23 February 1933, the formation of this unit was entrusted to Polizeimajor Wecke of the Prussian Police Force (during the early 1930s, police battalions were organised to protect and support Nazi leaders on political tours and during engagements). Two days later, Major Wecke reported that his police detachment for special purposes, with a strength of 14 officers and 400 men, had been established. On 17 July the detachment was officially retitled Landespolizei-gruppe (Land Police Group) *Wecke* z.b.V., becoming the first lan-despolizeigruppe in Germany. It was awarded a special land police standard by Göring on 13 September 1933, who stated: "It is my objective to transform the Prussian Police Force into a sharp-edged weapon, equal to the Reichswehr, which I can deliver to the Führer when the day comes for us to fight our exter-nal enemies." On 22 December 1933, the unit was again retitled, becoming the Landespolizei *General Göring*. Oberstleutnant Friedrich Jakoby, Göring's min-isterial adjutant, assumed command of the unit on 6 June 1933.

The Fallschirmjäger are born

The personnel of the Landespolizei *General Göring* initially served in a police capacity, but in March–April 1935 Göring reconstituted his Landespolizei *General Göring* to become the first fledgling airborne regiment. It was incorpo-rated into the new German Luftwaffe on 1 October of the same year, and train-ing commenced at Altengrabow. The landespolizeigruppe banner was retained as the official regimental banner, and a new *General Göring* sleeveband was established to wear on the lower right sleeve.

Hitler introduced general conscription on 16 March 1935, and on 1 April the Landespolizei *General Göring* adopted the more military designation of Regiment *General Göring*. In September, regimental commander Oberstleutnant Jakoby received the following order from Göring dated 23 September: "The Regiment *General Göring* [RGG] will be transferred into the Luftwaffe on 1 October 1935. From volunteers of the regiment, a Fallschirmschützen Bataillon [Parachute Soldiers Battalion] is to be established as a cadre for the future German Fallschirmtruppe [Parachute Troops]."

Below: *A Fallschirmjäger Knight's Cross general takes the salute during a wartime parade. As well as the Knight's Cross at his neck, he wears the German Cross in Gold on the right breast pocket. His footwear consists of riding boots, while his long cloth trousers sport broad white stripes and piping. This photograph is no later than the end of 1943, as in that year instructions were issued that senior Luftwaffe officers were no longer required to wear double, broad-cloth braided stripes on long cloth trousers.*

Left: *Army recruits get familiar with the parachute harness. There were two types of harness, the differences being slight. In the first, two shoulder webs crossed between the shoulder blades, with D-rings for attaching the pack just above the crossing point. The folded lengths of static line were stowed vertically on the pack. The second, and later, harness had a cloth shoulder yoke incorporating the shoulder webs, and the static lines were stowed horizontally on the pack.*

The *General Göring* Regiment was considered an élite unit and was paraded throughout Germany as an example for other military organisations to follow. After a demonstration parachute jump, during which the jumper injured himself and had to be carried off on a stretcher, sufficient officers and men – 600 – volunteered for parachute training. The amalgamation, in November 1935, of these 600 volunteers into the élite *General Göring* Regiment constituted the nucleus of the first German airborne battalion, and in January 1936 the Ist Jäger (Rifle) Battalion/RGG, commanded by Major Bruno Bräuer, and the 15th Engineer Company/RGG were transferred to training area Döberitz for parachute training, while the remainder of the regiment was sent to training area Altengrabow.

The official inauguration of the German paratroop arm dates from an Order of the Day signed by Inspector General of the Luftwaffe Erhard Milch on

Below: *Boarding the aircraft. Note the Feldwebel (Sergeant-Major), as denoted by the three stylised wings on his right arm. Instructions pertaining to the wearing of this new style of rank insignia were issued in December 1935. Note also the German national colours in diagonal bars of black over white over red in the shape of a shield on the helmets. Early versions of the latter were painted inside and out with a rust-preventing matt blue-grey paint. On the left side of the helmet was the silver-grey Luftwaffe eagle and swastika.*

Above: The final moments before the jump. As well as being extremely thorough, parachute training was also strict. During the descent, for example, singing or whistling was forbidden. After clipping his static line to the anchor line, the paratrooper launched himself from the aircraft by pushing against the hand rails and springing forward in one swift movement. Once the parachute opened the paratrooper, suspended by two straps attached to the back of his harness, had almost no control over his movements as he floated towards the ground.

Left: The jump. Unfortunately for the Fallschirmjäger, the RZ series of parachutes had the shrouds coming together at a single point behind and above the shoulder. The canopy and shrouds attached to the harness by a V-shaped rope strop joining this single point to D-rings behind the hips of the waist web. This meant an individual had to exit the aircraft in a spreadeagled position: if he fell in an upright position he would be flipped upside down, and his feet would tangle in the shroud lines. Normal jump height was around 121m (400ft).

Above: *Grinning Unteroffiziers (Sergeants) sprint away from their DFS 230 assault glider during a training exercise. Though the Soviets were the first to develop a military assault glider, the DFS 230 was the first to be used in combat. It was designed as a means of delivering an assault from the air without the troops having to store their weapons in containers.*

Right: *Another training shot, this time tackling enemy fortifications. While a Feldwebel (Sergeant-Major) provides covering fire with his MP 40 submachine gun, an Unteroffizier (Sergeant) climbs over the concrete and wire emplacement. For the attack on the Belgian fort of Eben Emael, intensive training was undertaken at Hildesheim, with full-sized mock-ups of the entire fort being built.*

Above: *After landing the men had to retrieve their weapons and ammunition from containers that had been dropped separately. Individual Fallschirmjäger dropped with a gas mask, handgun, four grenades, cartridge pouches, two rations bags and two canteens. Shown above is a two-man team with an MG 34 mounted on a tripod for the sustained fire role. During the first phase of an airborne operation the machine guns would provide defensive fire around the drop zone.*

Göring's behalf on 29 January 1936. This called for the recruitment of volunteers for parachute training at the Stendal Parachute Training School, 96km (60 miles) west of Berlin. The school had opened a few months after the institution of the Luftwaffe parachute units in January 1936. Both active and reserve personnel of the Luftwaffe were qualified to attend the Stendal Parachute Training School. On 5 November 1936 the Luftwaffe Parachutists' Badge was instituted. It was awarded to all officers, noncommissioned officers (NCOs) and other ranks of the Luftwaffe who had successfully completed six parachute jumps and other required tests. It was worn on the lower left breast to denote qualification as a military parachutist of the Luftwaffe. In order to retain the badge, it was necessary to requalify each year. In an order dated 2 May 1944, award of the badge was extended to medical, administrative and legal personnel who made a single combat jump. When the army parachute units were transferred to the Luftwaffe, qualified parachutists who had earned the Army Parachutists' Badge were required to retain the army badge. Members of the Waffen-SS assigned to the 500th, 501st or 502nd SS Parachute Battalions received the Luftwaffe Parachutists' Badge upon qualification.

In the mid-1930s, Göring and the Luftwaffe were not the only parties interested in the potential of airborne forces. The Oberkommando des Heeres (OKH) — Army High Command — quickly recognised the importance of parachute units

Left: *The MP 38/40 series of submachine guns first entered production in 1938. The Luftwaffe would eventually take over 195,000 of these weapons. Its compact size, making it easy to wield in close-quarter combat, made it popular with the Fallschirmjäger, and by the beginning of the war paratrooper units had an MP 38 (the MP 40 entered service in April 1940) for every fourth man. However, as this photograph illustrates, the ratio increased as the war progressed.*

to the success of the Blitzkrieg strategy (see Chapter 1), and had formed its own Schwere-Fallschirm-Infantrie-Kompanie (Heavy Parachute Infantry Company) in 1936 under the command of Major Richard Heidrich, a former tactics instructor at the Potsdam War School. The company took part with distinction in the autumn 1937 Wehrmacht military manoeuvres at Mecklenburg, becoming the star of the show and providing impetus for the consolidation of the German parachute arm. It was expanded and reorganised in the spring of 1938 into the second Fallschirmjäger battalion, and was organised like a support battalion with heavy machine guns and mortars. The Commander-in-Chief of the Army, Generaloberst Freiherr Werner von Fritsch, introduced the

Below: *Fallschirmjäger wearing the later pattern jump smock introduced in 1941. Manufactured from "splinter" camouflage material, it did not have step-in legs. The smock had two diagonal pocket openings on each side of the chest and two horizontal pocket openings at the front just below waist level. All the pockets were concealed by fly-fronted flaps. The smock also had a built-in holster at the back, on the right buttock, to hold a flare pistol.*

Army Parachutists' Badge on 1 September 1937. It was awarded to all members of the army's Parachute Infantry Battalion who had satisfactorily completed a parachute training course, which required the successful completion of six parachute jumps. Once qualified, individuals had to maintain their parachute skills by making a minimum of six jumps per year. However, the army's attempt to retain its own paratroop force was quashed by Göring, who brought all the Wehrmacht paratroopers under the control of the Luftwaffe (the army unit becoming the 2nd Battalion, 1st Parachute Regiment). When the battalion was transferred to the Luftwaffe on 1 January 1939 awards of this badge ceased. However, former recipients were authorised to continue wearing the badge in place of the Luftwaffe-pattern badge. Award of the army badge was resurrected again on 1 June 1943, with the only personnel on jump status being the 15th Light Company (Parachute Company), Brandenburg Division. This company sized unit was later enlarged to battalion size.

Roles on the ground

Quite apart from the continuing haggling between the army and the air force over jurisdiction, opinion was divided over Fallschirmjäger function. The Luftwaffe at this time believed in a policy of using paratroopers in small units as saboteurs behind enemy lines to disrupt enemy communications and morale, while the army felt they should be used in strength, almost like conventional infantry. In the end, exponents of both viewpoints were to see their ideas tested, and it is to the credit of the Fallschirmjäger and their instructors that they were able to fulfil both roles.

The next stage in the development of the Luftwaffe's paratroop arm, in July 1938, was the detachment of Bräuer's battalion from the *General Göring* Regiment. The Fallschirmjäger Batallion of the *General Göring* Regiment was

Above: *A paratrooper with a heavy cable drum on his back lays down a communications line. The first Fallschirm-Luftnachrichten-Abteilung (Parachute Signals Battalion) was formed in 1940 as part of the 7th Flieger Division. As the war progressed each parachute division had its own signals battalion. Each one had a total of 379 men and comprised one radio company, one telephone company and a light signals company. The First Parachute Army had an entire signals regiment, which was formed on 30 November 1943. It was commanded by Major Kurt Haumann and then Colonel Erich Leube.*

split from its original unit and became the Luftwaffe's new 1st Battalion, 1st Parachute Regiment. It was to be the nucleus of the new 7th Flieger Division under Major-General Kurt Student, who was ably assisted by Majors Gerhard Bassenge and Heinrich Trettner. The general was admirably suited for such an appointment, having served both as an infantryman and later as a fighter pilot and squadron leader during World War I. After the war he had been one of the staff officers closely involved with building up Germany's clandestine air force prior to Hitler's accession to power. Unlike many of his contemporaries, Student was both trusted by the Nazi hierarchy and liked by the men under his command. Although a Luftwaffe appointment, he was acceptable to the army because he disagreed with the air force's doctrine of using paratroops in "penny packets" as saboteurs. He was a tireless officer with great organisational ability whose ideas on the employment of airborne troops in a strategic capacity were revolutionary at the time.

The next few years saw the remainder of the *General Göring* Regiment, which now consisted of an infantry battalion, motorcycle company, engineer company and a light flak unit, evolve into the mighty Fallschirm Panzer Division *Hermann Göring*. As stated above, the army battalion became the 2nd Battalion, 1st Parachute Regiment, as part of Student's 7th Flieger Division.

Although the German occupation of the Sudetenland (the mountainous area between Bohemia and Silesia) in the autumn of 1938 did not require the use of military force, Student's new "division" took part as an exercise. Göring was so impressed by the outcome that army objections were overridden, and Heidrich's 2nd Battalion was amalgamated into the Luftwaffe. At the same

Below: *The paratrooper armed with the belt-fed MG 34 machine gun is an Obergefreiter (Corporal), as indicated by the double chevron rank insignia on his upper left sleeve midway between the elbow and the point of the shoulder. Originally each German parachute division had a machine-gun battalion made up of three companies, though this disappeared later in the war. The 1st Parachute Machine Gun Battalion went on to become a Korpstruppe (Corps Troop) with I Parachute Corps in January 1944, while the 2nd Parachute Machine Gun Battalion became a Korpstruppe with II Parachute Corps in May 1944.*

Above: *Fallschirmjäger with a 37mm Pak 35/36 antitank gun. This photograph was taken in 1944, when paratrooper divisions were fighting as ground units. Two uniform changes seen here reflect this role. First, hobnailed infantry marching boots have replaced Fallschirmjäger jump boots with their moulded rubber soles and heels (though front-lacing jump boots were also fitted with hobnails). Second, they are equipped with metal gas mask containers instead of the Fallschirmjäger canvas variety (which were designed to eliminate injury during a parachute drop).*

Left: *The LG40 recoilless gun was designed for airborne troops, having a range of 6.5km (four miles) and being able to knock out most enemy tanks then in service, though its backblast gave away its position. First used on Crete, its calibre was later increased from 75mm to 105mm. The LG40 was later replaced by the LG42, also in 105mm calibre, but the production of recoilless weapons ceased altogether in 1944.*

Right: *Training to knock out enemy tanks using a captured French Char S-35. Tanks were considered to be the main threat to lightly armed airborne troops once they had landed, and therefore a lot of time and effort went into devising tactics and weapons to deal with them.*

Above: *Another photograph from the same training exercise as the top photograph on this page. The first Fallschirmjäger antitank unit was formed in 1939 as the 7th Pak Kompanie (7th Antitank Company) for the 7th Flieger Division. In 1940 it was renamed the Fallschirm-Panzer-Jäger-Abteilung (Parachute Antitank Battalion), and in May 1943 became the Fallschirm-Panzer-Jäger-Abteilung 1 of the 1st Parachute Division. In January 1945 a number of Fallschirm-Panzer-Jagd-Bataillone (Parachute Tank Hunter Battalions) were also established but they saw relatively little service before the war ended.*

time, in January 1939, instructions were issued for the raising of a second regiment, and Heidrich's pride was salved by promoting him to command this unit. Both regiments were to be operational by the time of the Norwegian campaign in the spring of the following year. They were organised along standard infantry lines, with each regiment comprising three battalions (though in 1940 the 2nd Parachute Regiment only had two) and each battalion having four companies.

Though Germany's airborne forces were now under the control of the Luftwaffe, the differences of opinion between the army and air force as to their employment continued. The army saw their role as being akin to what General Mitchell had proposed in World War I: the landing of a large body of men behind enemy lines to carry out conventional infantry attacks in the enemy's rear. To this end the 22nd Infantry Division was selected and trained for air-landing operations. For its part the Luftwaffe continued to advocate commando-type units which would attack and destroy important targets. Basing its training around that premise, it laid stress on military engineering skills, particularly demolitions.

Above: *A posed photograph showing an attack on a bunker with handguns! Both these men are wearing the Luftwaffe flying service blouse (Fliegerbluse). The four "eagles" and braiding on the collar patch of the paratrooper nearest the camera indicates he is an Oberfeldwebel (Warrant Officer). Both these men have seen action, as indicated by the ribbon of the Iron Cross on their blouses.*

The debate continues

When the two parachute arms of service amalgamated, each submitted its own evaluation of airborne techniques and employment to the Armed Forces High Command (OKW). The latter, having weighed up the evidence, then issued a directive in 1938 which did nothing to resolve the divergence of opinion. The directive stressed two types of airborne mission. First, there were strategic air-landing missions carried out in conjunction with the army: "The scope and execution of an airlanding operation depends upon both the military situation and the intention behind the operation. In addition to the airlanded troops, other Luftwaffe units, fighters and fighter-bombers are to be employed. This type of mission must be closely linked to army operations. The Luftwaffe will be responsible for the preparation and execution of the battle plan as well as for air supply drops. The army will only assume command of airlanded formations once contact has been established between those men and our own ground forces." Second, airlanding operations within the framework of a Luftwaffe mission: "In this connection what is implied are sabotage or demolition units landed onto objectives which have been nominated by the Luftwaffe because it had not been possible to totally destroy or severely damage them by aerial bombardment."

While the conceptual differences were being discussed, there was a continuing expansion of the airborne force and amalgamations of its units until a point was reached at which the disparate groups needed to be formed into a single major formation. On 1 July 1938, the Oberkommando der Luftwaffe (OKL) – Luftwaffe High Command – ordered that the parachute, glider and air transport units under its command be combined into the 7th Flieger Division. Tempelhof in Berlin became the headquarters for the new formation and Student was designated its commander.

Airlift capacity

Despite Student's drive and the fact that the building of German airborne forces was pushed forward as quickly as possible, by the outbreak of World War II neither the 7th Flieger Division nor the 22nd Division were at full strength. The roles and purposes of the two formations were as follows: the 22nd Division was a conventional army infantry formation whose regiments would be transported to the target in Junkers Ju 52 aircraft. There was sufficient aircraft on the strength of 7th Flieger Division's Special Operations Air Transport Group to move 5000 men in a single lift. The operational method was for the aircraft to land units of the 22nd on airfields behind enemy lines which had been captured by paratroops and/or glider units. Once the soldiers

Below: *Preparing mortar shells for an 80mm Granatwerfer 34, though to be precise it is probably for the kurzer 80mm Granatwerfer 42 (kz 80mm GrW 42), which was developed for the Fallschirmjäger and other special forces. This was a short-barrelled version of the GrW 34, being lighter and more compact, which reduced its range to 1100m (3660ft). From 1944 the 1st, 2nd, 3rd, 4th, 5th, 6th, 7th, 9th and 20th Parachute Divisions had their own Fallschirm-Granatwerfer-Bataillone (Parachute Mortar Battalions). Each battalion consisted of three companies, each of which was equipped with the larger 120mm mortar (the German 120mm GrW 42 was a copy of the Soviet 120 PM-38, and 8461 had been produced by March 1945).*

of the 22nd Division had deplaned, they would operate as conventional infantry. The parachute-trained units of the 7th Flieger Division would be landed by parachute or brought in by glider.

Fallschirmjäger training was vigorous and tough, emphasised by Hitler's own "10 commandments to the Fallschirmjäger", the first of which stated: "You are the chosen fighting men of the Wehrmacht. You will seek combat and train yourselves to endure all hardships. Battle shall be your fulfilment." One commandment was typically Hitlerite: "Against an open foe, fight with chivalry, but extend no quarter to a guerrilla." All recruits to the Fallschirmjäger were volunteers, both before and during the war, which meant they responded well to arduous training and maintained a high level of morale throughout the course. All volunteers had to be relatively lightweight – 85kg (187lb) – and not suffer from dizziness or air sickness. Recruits had to have no fear of heights, which was tested by making individuals jump from a height of 15.2m (50ft) into water. Next, they were taken aboard aircraft for flight testing, during which they were given a "feel of the air" and to determine whether they suffered from air sickness or not. Throughout the induction process instructors looked for courage, initiative and intelligence in recruits.

Fallschirmjäger training

The training course itself lasted eight weeks, divided between four weeks of ground training and four weeks of airborne training. During the latter period each recruit would be required to make six jumps, after which he would qualify for the Parachutist Qualification Badge (it was usual, in those early days, for

Above: *A Fallschirmjäger MG 34 team on an exercise (note the temporary cloth bands worn over the plain grey-green helmet covers). The metal boxes containing belts of 7.92mm ammunition for the weapon were dropped in containers and had to be retrieved at the drop zone. The MG 34 weighed 11.42kg (25lb) and had a cyclic rate of fire of 900 rounds per minute. When fired from a tripod it had an effective range of 3500m (11,655ft).*

Right: *Under observation during a field exercise (note the observers in the top right-hand corner of the photograph). Heinrich Hermsen, a Fallschirmjäger volunteer, describes weapons training: "On 20 July 1942, I reported at Stendal and, two days later, was sent with my comrades to a place near Tangerhütte, in Weissenwarthe, for basic training. In early October 1942, after being trained in using the 98K, P38 and the MG 34, the Parachute Depot and Training Regiment was posted to Russia."*

Below: *Of interest in this photograph is the spare barrel for the MG 34 carried in the case on the back of the paratrooper in the foreground. In combat the MG 34 required numerous barrel changes: usually after every 250 rounds of burst fire. The weapon had a muzzle velocity of 755mps (2514fps).*

the paratrooper to be armed only with a pistol and hand grenades; other weapons were carried in containers which were dropped at the same time as the soldiers). During the war years, training for parachute qualification was relegated to regimental training schools where personnel were instructed in parachute techniques and eventual qualification. However, fuel and aircraft became more scarce as the war progressed and qualification became more difficult (there was also little time for training as manpower demands increased). For example, Generalmajor Heinrich Trettner, commander of the 4th Parachute Division, did not attend parachute school, and was thus not awarded the Parachutists' Badge.

Above: *Hitler poses with the Knight's Cross winners of the Eben Emael operation. On the Führer's right is Walter Koch, while to Koch's right is Rudolf Witzig.*

VINDICATION

The Blitzkrieg campaigns in Europe in 1939–40 were to prove that the Fallschirmjäger could play a vital part in the Germany Army's plans. Though they saw limited action in Poland, Student's men were to prove their worth in Scandinavia and would be pivotal in giving Hitler victory over the British and French in May 1940, when they unlocked Holland and Belgium's defence lines.

Left: *Flushed with victory, Hauptmann Walter Koch takes stock at the end of the campaign in the West. Koch led the Fallschirmjäger detachment that took the fortress of Eben Emael and key Belgian bridges over the Albert Canal in an assault at the beginning of May 1940.*

At the end of August 1939, the 7th Flieger Division was far from complete. True, rifle battalions and divisional troops had been added to the formation, but it would not be until after the campaign in the West in 1940 that it would approach full strength.

The German Blitzkrieg was unleashed on Poland on 1 September 1939. By the second day the Polish Air Force had been destroyed on the ground, and Germany's panzers were streaming east. The combination of surprise, speed and terror tactics destroyed the Polish armed forces of 3,000,000 men at a cost of 10,000 German dead. Warsaw surrendered on 27 September and the last Polish troops ceased fighting on 6 October. Though the Fallschirmjäger were briefed for a number of airborne missions, the speed of the German advance made such operations superfluous. Nevertheless, elements of the 2nd and 3rd Battalions of the 1st Parachute Regiment engaged Polish troops in a number of small but hard-fought ground actions between 14 and 24 September. In addition, troops

Right: *German paratroopers drift to the ground during the attack on Norway in April 1940. The following Fallschirmjäger units were committed to the Norwegian campaign: Headquarters and 1st Battalion, 1st Parachute Regiment (Hauptmann Walther); 1st Company, 1st Parachute Regiment (Oberleutnant Schmidt); 2nd Company, 1st Parachute Regiment (Hauptmann Gröschke); 3rd Company, 1st Parachute Regiment (Oberleutnant von Brandis); and 2nd Battalion, 2nd Parachute Regiment (Hauptmann Pietzonka).*

Below: *Fallschirmjäger exit a Junkers Ju 52 over Norway. For the Danish and Norwegian campaigns the Luftwaffe deployed over 100 bombers and 60 fighters to ensure German air superiority. Part of Destroyer Squadron 76, consisting of eight Messerschmitt Bf 110s, was allocated to support parachute units in Norway. During the assault on Fornebu airfield, located on a small peninsula west of Oslo, the paras were forced to abort their drop due to poor visibility. However, the Bf 110s, nearly out of fuel, landed on the airfield and used their machine guns against the defenders as the follow-on airlanding troops came in.*

of the 2nd Parachute Regiment also fought in Poland, seeing action at Deblin and the Dukla Pass. Following the Polish surrender all paratroopers returned to their depots in Germany.

Hitler next turned his attention to Norway and Denmark. Germany's iron ore came via two sources: via the Baltic Sea and down the coast from Narvik in northern Norway. The British Royal Navy had established a naval blockade that threatened the latter route. German possession of Norway would not only allow land-based aircraft to be used against the blockade, but would also provide a springboard for aerial attacks against the British Isles themselves. The invasions of Denmark and Norway were carried out with great daring, and not a little audacity. An example of the latter occurred in February 1940, when a German transport aircraft landed at Fornebu airport in Norway. Around 30 passengers disembarked and began taking photographs, making sketches and writing notes. This episode, which took place at the height of the so-called

Altmark incident (when British warships violated Norwegian neutrality to capture a German vessel holding British prisoners), went almost unnoticed. But the intelligence gathered was later put to good use.

The invasion of the two countries began on 9 April 1940, the aim being to overwhelm resistance by bold initial strikes and to quickly seize airfields and ports to deny any Allied assistance to the two states. Throughout, the campaign was characterised by excellent army, navy and air force cooperation, though interestingly it violated the principle of concentration and invited the German forces to be defeated in detail (though only if the Allies could react quickly). Denmark and Norway had to be attacked simultaneously because the use of Denmark's air bases and the control of her coastal waters would facilitate the occupation of Norway.

Above: *Fallschirmjäger land outside Narvik in May 1940. The 1st, 2nd, 3rd and 4th Companies of the 1st Parachute Regiment jumped into the town, along with 200 men of the 137th Regiment of the 3rd Mountain Division who had undergone a crash parachute course at the Wittstock parachute school. Among the mountain troops was Eugen Meindl, who transferred to the Luftwaffe on 28 November 1940 and finished the war as the commander of II Parachute Corps.*

The first Fallschirmjäger drops

The first airborne operations of the war were carried out by men of the 1st Battalion, 1st Parachute Regiment, under the command of Major Erich Walther. The objectives in Denmark were seized effortlessly: one company (the 4th Company under the command of Hauptmann Walther Gericke) less a platoon dropped to seize the Vordingborg bridge linking Copenhagen with its ferry terminal; the remaining platoon parachuted onto the two airfields at Aalborg and secured them without a fight. The next day Denmark surrendered. Things went less smoothly for the paratroopers in Norway, though.

The 2nd Company was ordered to take Fornebu airfield near Oslo and hold it until troops of the 163rd Infantry Division could be airlanded. The 3rd Company, commanded by Oberleutnant von Brandis, was ordered to secure the Sola airfield at Stavanger. At Fornebu thick fog obscured the target and the paratroopers had to abort the drop. By the time the transport aircraft carrying the airlanding units reached the airfield the fog had started to clear and they were able to land. They suffered heavy casualties but took the objective. At Sola the paratroopers successfully dropped close to the airfield. Though they met resistance they secured the airfield with the assistance of fighter-bombers, and

the airfield was ready to receive Ju 52s containing infantry within 20 minutes of the airborne assault. The most costly Fallschirmjäger operation in the Norwegian campaign involved the 1st Company under the command of Oberleutnant Herbert Schmidt, which was dropped 144km (90 miles) north of Oslo. The men landed among strong Norwegian defensive positions and took heavy casualties, including Schmidt himself. Surrounded and fighting in appalling weather conditions, the Fallschirmjäger were forced to surrender after four days when their ammunition ran out.

Notwithstanding this setback, the Blitzkrieg in Norway had been a stunning success, and by 5 May the Germans under the overall command of General Nikolaus von Falkenhorst occupied the whole of southern Norway. Though French and British forces had been landed at Namsos, Andalsnes and Narvik, the German attack against France and the Low Countries which began on 10

May 1940 made the Norwegian deployment a luxury the Allies could ill afford. The last Fallschirmjäger operation in Norway was undertaken by a battalion of the 1st Parachute Regiment, when it was dropped into Narvik to reinforce General Dietl's besieged forces located there. A few days later the 137th Regiment of the German 3rd Mountain Division was dropped around Narvik following a crash-course in parachute jumping. There were a number of jump injuries and a wide dispersion on the ground, but amazingly most of the men linked up with the German forces at Narvik. Dietl withdrew from Narvik at the end of May, but between 7–9 June the Allies pulled their forces out of the town, and by 9 June Norway had been cleared of all organised Allied resistance. The Germans had seized a state of three million people in a campaign that had lasted two months. The campaign had also demonstrated to the world the viability of using small parachute detachments to seize airfields as a prelude to the landing of large numbers of troops from aircraft.

The greatest success of Germany's parachute arm was arguably the campaign in the West in May 1940. Though only comprising one division — 7th Flieger Division — the skilful use of the airborne troops played a large part in the German victory. In fact, Hitler's armies were inferior in numbers to those

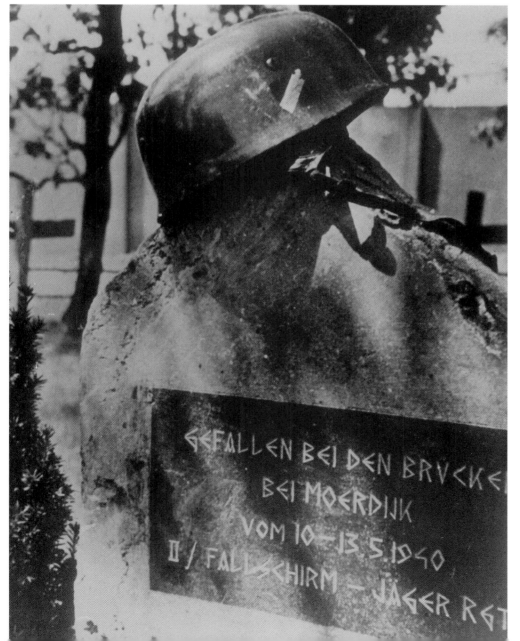

Left: *Commemorative plaque to the men of the 2nd Battalion, 1st Parachute Regiment, for their actions in the Moerdijk sector in May 1940. Fallschirmjäger success in holding the bridge was imperative, as Student stated after the war: "The limitations of our strength compelled us to concentrate on two objectives – the points which seemed the most essential to the success of the invasion. The main effort, under my own control, was directed against the bridges of Rotterdam, Dordrecht and Moerdijk by which the main route from the south was carried across the mouths of the Rhine. Our task was to capture the bridges before the Dutch could blow them up, and keep them open."*

opposing them, and he had fewer tanks and less powerful ones than his opponents had. Only in the air were his forces superior. But the campaign would be decided by only a fraction of his units – 10 armoured divisions, one parachute division and one airlanding division – out of the 130 which the Wehrmacht had for the campaign. A vital part of the German attack was an assault against key points in the defences of Holland and Belgium, which would focus the Allies' attention away from the main thrust: through the wooded country of the Ardennes. To make the secondary threat convincing and lure the British and French to the Belgians' aid, the Germans would have to overcome the Belgian and Dutch defences. To do so Student only had 4500 trained paratroopers. Of these, 4000 were used against Holland and the rest against Belgium. The key to cracking the defences in Belgium were the bridges over the Albert Canal and the fortress of Eben Emael, which was constructed of concrete and steel and whose artillery dominated the whole area. Against Holland Student deployed the majority of his 7th Flieger Division and General Graf von Sponeck's 22nd Airlanding Division. Dutch defences rested on three successive lines: a lightly fortified delay-

Above: *A burning Ju 52 over Holland. General von Sponeck was due to land at Ypenburg, but due to heavy antiaircraft fire he flew on to Ockenburg. The Fallschirmjäger allocated to drop on these two airfields landed too far south of their targets, thus the airlanding troops were the first to engage the defenders. The wrecked aircraft at Ockenburg meant follow-on troops had to land away from the targets and then march some distance to fight the enemy.*

Left: *Dutch soldiers on a downed Ju 52 north of Rotterdam. Von Sponeck's 22nd Airlanding Division had a hard time of it in Holland. The Ju 52s carrying troops of the 47th Infantry Regiment, for example, landed at Valkenburg in the face of heavy fire, and, as can be seen, the aircraft sank to their axles in the soft mud.*

Above: *A Ju 52 shot down near Ypenburg, where 11 of the 13 Junkers carrying the first assault company of the 65th Regiment were downed by antiaircraft fire. Student committed 4000 of his men against Holland in four waves. First wave: Headquarters of the 1st Parachute Regiment plus a signals squad dropped in the Tweede Tol sector. Second wave: 1st Battalion, 1st Parachute Regiment, jumped to take the Dordrecht bridges. Third wave: 2nd Battalion, 1st Parachute Regiment, jumped to take the two Moerdijk bridges. Fourth wave: 3rd Battalion, 1st Parachute Regiment, dropped onto Waalhaven airport; 7th Sturm-Geschütz-Batterie (7th Assault Gun Battery) airlanded onto Waalhaven, then Moerdijk and Dordrecht; 7th Sanitäts-Kompanie (7th Medical Company) airlanded at Waalhaven and jumped near Rotterdam; 1st Battalion, 2nd Parachute Regiment, jumped over Ypenburg, Ockenburg and Valkenburg airfields; 3rd Company, 2nd Parachute Regiment, jumped over The Hague; 2nd Battalion, 2nd Parachute Regiment, airlanded at Waalhaven; and 6th Company, 2nd Parachute Regiment, jumped over Valkenburg airfield and fought at Katwijk.*

ing position at the border; the main "Grebbe-Peel line", which made use of natural defensive barriers; and "Fortress Holland" – Rotterdam, Amsterdam, Utrecht and The Hague – which was protected by estuaries, rivers and flooded areas.

Bearing in mind that there had never been a large-scale airborne operation in warfare before, Student may have been tempted to minimise risks by using his men to support the ground attack directly. However, what he proposed was radical: to use his men to crack open "Fortress Holland" and paralyse the nerve centres of the Dutch government, thereby destroying the Dutch will to continue fighting. Though this plan was opposed by Luftwaffe Chief of Staff Jeschonnek, it was approved by a delighted Hitler.

Student's plan

The operation against Holland had two elements. First, von Sponeck's division would land at the airfields at Valkenburg, Ockenburg and Ypenburg after they had been taken by parachute assault, then two infantry regiments would enter The Hague and capture the government and royal family, or at least disrupt Dutch defence plans. Second, south of Rotterdam Student's division would land by parachute to seize crossings over the major water obstacles that protected "Fortress Holland's" southern flank. An infantry regiment would also airland at Waalhaven to provide a reserve.

The campaign in the West began on 10 May, and wherever the Fallschirmjäger landed in Holland they encountered stiff resistance from a Dutch Army determined to defend its country. However, Student's well-trained men captured all but one of their objectives, and the unit that landed at Waalhaven captured the bridge intact. Paratroopers landed in Rotterdam's football stadium, and then advanced and captured the Meuse bridge. The Dordrecht and Moerdijk bridges were captured intact and held in the face of heavy resistance. After two days the leading panzers of General Georg von Küchler's Eighteenth Army reached the intact Moerdijk bridge – "Fortress Holland" had been cracked.

Right: *The attack on Eben Emael. Sappers cross the ditch in front of the fort in a dinghy on the morning of 11 May. Preparations for the assault were intensive. Assault Detachment Koch had been formed in November 1939 and was cut off from the outside world while it trained for its attack against the fortress.*

Below: *The Albert Canal was integrated into Belgium's defences, and at Eben Emael was used to fill the ditch in front of the fortress. To unlock those defences Koch's assault group comprised: Granit Group (Oberleutnant Witzig) – 85 paratroopers in 11 gliders to take Eben Emael; Eisen Group (Leutnant Schächter) – 90 paratroopers in 10 gliders to take Cannes bridge; Beton Group (Oberleutnant Schacht) – 122 paratroopers in 11 gliders to take Vroenhoven bridge; and Stahl Group (Oberleutnant Altmann) – 92 paratroopers in 10 gliders to take Veldvezelt bridge.*

Left: *One of Eben Emael's knocked-out emplacements. Within the first 10 minutes of the assault Witzig's gliderborne men had successfully attacked nine of the fort's installations. The Fallschirmjäger used a combination of small arms, explosives and flamethrowers to overcome the defenders, plus courage in large amounts.*

Below: *Fallschirmjäger flamethrowers in action at Eben Emael. By the evening of 10 May Witzig's men had consolidated their position, and by 07:00 hours the next morning the advance section of the 51st Sapper Battalion had linked up with the paratroopers and the defenders had surrendered.*

Von Sponeck's 22 Division had a tougher time north of Rotterdam. He had just enough paratroopers to take the three airfields, and only 15 minutes between the parachute drops and the arrival of Junkers bringing in his infantry. Things began to go wrong from the start. The flat, patchwork landscape confused the pilots, who dropped the paratroopers wide of their objectives. Thus when the Junkers touched down at Valkenburg they did so in the face of intense fire. The aircraft got bogged down in soft sand and couldn't be moved, thus successive waves had to turn back. At Ypenburg, 11 of the 13 Junkers carrying the first assault company of the 65th Regiment were shot down by antiaircraft fire. Wrecks of aircraft littered the ground at Ockenburg, where a similar story unfolded. Nevertheless, enough troops had been landed to adversely affect Dutch morale and contribute to their surrender on 14 May.

The fortress of Eben Emael and the bridges over the Albert Canal had to be taken to allow the advancing German Sixth Army to pass unhindered into Belgium. Student later wrote: "The Albert Canal venture was Hitler's own idea. I used 500 men under Captain Koch. The commander of the Sixth Army, General von Reichenau, and his chief of staff General Paulus, both capable generals, regarded the undertaking as an adventure in which they had no faith." A parachute assault against Eben Emael had been ruled out due to the limited space and the chance of some men missing the drop zone. It was thus carried out in gliders. The attack on the fortress and bridges was planned and practised in utmost secrecy.

The assignment went to Hauptmann Walter Koch, who was to form a Parachute Assault Detachment from men of his 1st Battalion, 1st Parachute Regiment, and Oberleutnant Rudolf Witzig's pioneer company from the 2nd Battalion, 1st Parachute Regiment. Group Granite would assault the fortress. This

Above: *Paratroopers photographed after the fall of Eben Emael. The bridges at Vroenhoven and Veltvezelt were captured intact by the Fallschirmjäger and defended successfully before being relieved by German infantry during the afternoon of 10 May. At Cannes the Belgians blew up the bridge, and the paratroopers spent the whole of 10 May fighting off enemy attacks. The man above in a suit is a Brandenburger, one of a number of specially trained soldiers who seized key points ahead of the main German attack.*

unit consisted of two officers and 83 men, 11of whom were glider pilots. Group Granite's 11 gliders and their Ju 52 tows took off from two airfields outside Cologne at 04:30 hours on the morning of 10 May 1940. They were released inside German territory and were left to glide to their target. Only nine gliders landed on top of Eben Emael at 05:20 hours, the other two, including Witzig's, had to abort shortly after take-off and land back in Germany. Witzig later reached the target with a new tow.

Success at Eben Emael

The defenders were taken completely by surprise, which turned to consternation when the paratroopers started to blow open the gun emplacements with hollow-charge explosives. They blasted their way through the concrete, disabled the guns and neutralised the garrison.

Meanwhile, paratroop drops secured the bridges at Vroenhoven, Cannes and Veldvezelt with relatively small losses, thereby breaching the Belgian defence line and allowing the Sixth Army's units to pour across. The breakthrough in Belgium was not the decisive stroke in the campaign in the West, but it had a vital effect: it drew the Allies' attention in the wrong direction and attracted the most mobile part of their forces to the area, which meant they could not be deployed to meet the greater threat that then developed in the south.

For the Fallschirmjäger the campaign had been a vindication of their doctrine and training. This was especially true in Belgium, where on the entire invasion front the bridges were blown up by the defenders except where airborne troops were used. But the campaign had an unhappy footnote. General Student and his staff had flown to the captured Waalhaven airfield and had then proceeded into Rotterdam on 14 May, where he conducted peace negotiations before the Dutch capitulation on the same day. It was during these negotiations that Student suffered a non-fatal gunshot wound to the head inflicted by a passing unit of the *SS Leibstandarte Adolf Hitler*, which was unaware of the surrender and raced into the city firing wildly at all and sundry. And as the Dutch were signing the surrender terms, Rotterdam was bombed due to a breakdown in communication between ground forces and the Luftwaffe. Nevertheless, the campaign in the West had been a resounding triumph for Hilter's sky warriors.

Below: *Hitler congratulates his Fallschirmjäger after the Eben Emael success. Rudolf Witzig, who won a Knight's Cross for his part in the attack, later stated the reasons for the victory: "although an attack was clearly not expected, our use of tactical and technical surprise made the destruction of the vital surface installations, artillery and observation posts possible, and this in turn made the enemy uncertain about the general situation." He also provided a telling insight into the enemy's psychological state: "Belgium had been weakened by neutralistic politics, and an ill-prepared army fought badly because it was badly led. For the most part it lacked the will to fight."*

Above: *Ju 52s drop Fallschirmjäger during the conquest of Crete. Note the four-parachute clusters, indicating the dropping of heavy equipment, such as motorcycles and field guns.*

THE INVASION OF CRETE

The conquest of Crete stands as a lasting tribute to the professionalism, courage and tenacity of Germany's airborne forces. But victory was bought at a heavy price, and when the battle was over a shocked Führer, who was not usually unduly worried by losses, forbade any more large-scale airborne operations.

Left: *After the fighting on Crete is over, Fallschirmjäger discuss the battle with a soldier from Ringel's 5th Gebirgs (Mountain) Division who also fought in Operation "Mercury". Note the Gebirgsjäger Edelweiss badge on his upper right sleeve, indicating that he is a qualified mountaineer.*

Following the successful conclusion of the campaign in the West, Hitler turned his attention to the East: the invasion and conquest of the Soviet Union. Before he could so, though, he needed to secure his southern flank. Hungary and Romania were German satellites, and by using severe diplomatic pressure Hitler was able to bring Yugoslavia into the Axis alliance. However, the deployment of 57,000 British troops to Greece encouraged an anti-German coup in Yugoslavia in late March 1941, and thus the Führer was forced into a Balkan campaign. For the airborne forces it would mean their biggest and most celebrated operation. But beforehand they would carry out a smaller operation that was a complete success.

The Germans invaded Yugoslavia and Greece on 6 April 1941, and immediately the Blitzkrieg began to sweep all before it. In Greece, by mid-April, the German Army was advancing in three columns: one from Larissa, one through Thebes towards Elensia and Athens, and the third from Larissa and Arta

Left: *The German drop on the Corinth Canal on 26 April 1941. The mission was entrusted to the 1st Battalion, 2nd Parachute Regiment (Hauptmann Kroh); 2nd Battalion, 2nd Parachute Regiment (Hauptmann Pietzonka); 13th and 14th Companies of the 2nd Parachute Regiment; an engineer squad; 7th Artillery Battery; 1st Company, 7th Parachute Medical Battalion; and the 7th Airlanding Company (gliders). The drop was supported by two squadrons of Messerschmitt Bf 110s, which strafed British forces on the ground. However, when the Ju 52s approached the target they still flew into heavy antiaircraft fire from both banks of the canal.*

towards Lepanto. Greek resistance had all but collapsed and the British under General Maitland Wilson were withdrawing through the Corinthian Isthmus towards the Peloponnesus. The Corinthian Isthmus is cut by a canal whose sides are deep and steep. It was decided to capture the Corinthian pass to establish a bridgehead to assist the crossing of German ground troops and cut off the British retreat.

The Fallschirmjäger units assigned to the mission were two battalions of the 2nd Parachute Regiment, reinforced by one parachute engineer platoon, artillery and one parachute medical company. On 25 April, more than 400 Ju

Below: *Fallschirmjäger fight Allied troops at Corinth. Though over 2000 British and Greek troops were taken prisoner in the operation, the drop went in too late to block the escape route of the British Expeditionary Force.*

52s and numerous gliders were transferred from the Plovdiv area in Bulgaria to the airfield at Larissa. The drop was scheduled for 07:00 hours on 26 April.

The aircraft flew over the Pindus Mountains and dropped to an altitude of 45.7m (150ft) over the Gulf of Corinth, which was covered in a haze that masked their approach. The pilots pulled up to a height of 122m (400ft), reduced speed and released their loads above the objectives. The first to land were the gliders, which touched down on both sides of the isthmus. The parachute troops jumped at the same time, landed north of the canal, seized the bridge and captured a large number of British troops in the process.

Right: *One of Student's machine gunners in Greece in 1941. The Fallschirmjäger had displayed their usual daring in the campaign, and not a little bluff. The commander of the 2nd Parachute Regiment's 2nd Company, for example, Leutnant Hans Teusen, landed by glider and stormed into Corinth. Subsequently ordered towards Nauplia in pursuit of the retreating British, once he had caught up with them Teusen, vastly outnumbered, persuaded the British commander that he was the vanguard of an entire division. His powers of persuasion resulted in over 1200 British soldiers surrendering, and him being awarded a Knight's Cross.*

The aim of seizing the bridge intact had been achieved, but then a stray anti-aircraft shell detonated the demolition charges on the structure after German engineers had cut the detonating cord. The bridge blew up, killing several paratroopers in the process. However, on the same day engineers constructed a temporary span adjacent to the one that had been destroyed to allow traffic between the mainland and the Peloponnesus to flow unhindered. If the drop had been made earlier, large numbers of the British Expeditionary Force (which had completed its evacuation by 27 April) would have been trapped.

Objective – Crete

After the fall of Greece all eyes turned to Crete. For both sides the island was of importance: for the British to maintain naval supremacy in the eastern Mediterranean from the base at Suda, while for the Germans Crete would provide an ideal forward base for offensive air and naval operations in the Mediterranean. It would be able to support Axis ground offensives in Egypt, and its capture would deny Allied aircraft potential bases for striking at Germany's Ploesti oil fields in Romania.

General Student, commander of XI Flieger (Air) Corps, had advocated using the whole of Germany's airborne forces to take Crete and Cyprus. Oberstleutnant Freiherr von der Heydte, who fought on Crete, relates the story: "This suggestion was submitted to Göring by the Commander-in-Chief

Below: *British troops arrive on Crete after their evacuation from Greece. Though most soldiers had their personal weapons with them, they were short of tents, blankets, cooking facilities and greatcoats (the nights were very cold). The defences of the island were wanting on the eve of the German attack: not only was the garrison inadequate to resist a major assault, Freyberg's aerial assets were hopelessly outnumbered. In recognition of this, he had ordered his aircraft off the island on 19 May. However, he was not permitted to make the airfields unfit to land aircraft on as it was hoped they might be used later. They were – by the Germans!*

Above: *Suda under Stuka attack on the morning of 20 May 1941. Fighters and bombers preceded the Fallschirmjäger, Bf 109s strafing the coastal strip between Maleme and Canea, making it hazardous for ground troops to move from their slit trenches. The Luftwaffe's VIII Flieger Corps deployed a total of 610 fighters and bombers to support the airborne operation.*

of Luftflotte IV [General Alexander Löhr] — under whose command was General Student — on 15 April, and Göring ordered General Student to report to him on 20 April. On 21 April Hitler saw Student, and on 25 April Directive 28 ordered the immediate preparation of Operation *Merkur* — the surprise attack on Crete."

All units to take part in the operation were assembled within two weeks. However, because of logistical problems the date of the attack was put back to 20 May. For the attack Student deployed 500 Ju 52 aircraft and 80 DFS 230 gliders to airlift the attacking forces from the airfields in Greece. The assault force consisted of the Luftlande-Sturmregiment (Airlanding Assault Regiment)

Right: *Then the Fallschirmjäger went in. Despite the preliminary air bombardment, the paratroopers encountered intense enemy fire as soon as they left their aircraft. Many of the Ju 52s were damaged by ground fire and were unable to airlift the second wave. At Maleme, many paratroopers were killed during their descent, and because of the volume of enemy fire those who did survive the jump were unable to reach the weapons containers. This meant they had to fight with what they dropped with: handguns and hand grenades.*

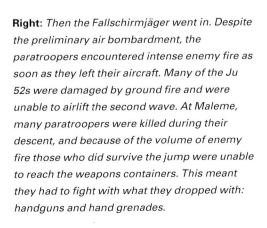

Above: *A Ju 52 in flames over Crete. An indication of the losses in transport aircraft suffered by XI Flieger Corps can be ascertained from the comments of Hauptmann Shirmer, 2nd Battalion, 2nd Parachute Regiment, who was in the second wave dropped at Retimo: "Many of the aircraft which had delivered the first wave early on 20 May were so badly damaged that they could not return to base. Consequently, only 29 Ju 52s were available to deliver the battalion instead of the 54 that were expected."*

under Generalmajor Meindl, 7th Flieger Division (Generalleutnant Süssmann) and the 5th Mountain Division (Generalmajor Ringel). The latter replaced the 22nd Airlanding Division, which could not be transferred in time from Romania, and was in any case guarding the Ploesti oil fields.

Crete itself is 256km (160 miles) long and between 12.8–56km (8–35 miles) wide. The interior of the island is barren and covered by eroded mountains. Water is scarce and roads are few. The only usable port on the south coast is at Sfakia. The main towns on the island are in the north: Maleme, Canea, Retimo and Heraklion. For the Royal Navy, the only adequate port was in Suda Bay, also in the north.

Risk assessment

The original Luftwaffe plan proposed airborne landings in the western part of the island between the airfield at Maleme and Canea (the location of various bridges, roads and antiaircraft positions), followed by an eastward thrust. It meant German airborne forces could concentrate within a small area and achieve local air and ground superiority relatively quickly. The main disadvantage was that it

Right: *Many Fallschirmjäger were dropped in the wrong locations. The 4th Company and headquarters of the Luftlande-Sturmregiment landed in the middle of a British position; only the 9th Company of Major Heilmann's 3rd Battalion, 3rd Parachute Regiment, landed in the right place. It soon became apparent to Student that the first wave had taken none of its main objectives, while several battalion and company commanders had been killed, in addition to Generalleutnant Süssmann.*

Right: *Maleme airfield – the key to winning the battle for Crete. By the end of the first day Student had been receiving news of nothing but failure. Only at Maleme was there a glimmer of hope. The 3rd Parachute Regiment had secured neither Canea nor Galatas; the 2nd Parachute Regiment had captured a hill overlooking Retimo airfield, but had taken heavy casualties doing so; and the 1st Parachute Regiment had been widely dispersed on landing and was in no position to take Heraklion airfield. For the 7000 paratroopers who had been committed, the immediate future appeared bleak indeed. This photograph was taken after the battle for Crete was over, and shows British bombs exploding on the airfield.*

Below: *At Maleme the Fallschirmjäger had invested, though not secured, the airfield. The key to taking the air base was Hill 107, which overlooked the airfield and dominated the surrounding terrain. This photograph shows the Ju 52s that brought in the German mountain troops and their equipment, and was taken after the battle for the airfield had ended.*

might lead to extensive mountain fighting, and the enemy would remain in possession of the Heraklion and Retimo airfields to the east. The plan of XI Flieger Corps advocated simultaneous parachute drops at seven points, including Maleme, Canea, Retimo and Heraklion. This plan had the advantage of capturing all strategic points on the island at once. A subsequent mopping-up operation would clear the rest of the island. However, the operation was risky because the units dropped would be dispersed over a wide area, making them vulnerable to counterattacks. The plan involved Student's so-called "oil spot tactics", whereby

a number of small airheads would be created in the area to be attacked, at first without any point of main effort. These airheads would be continually reinforced until they finally linked up. A post-war German assessment of airborne operations described how they nearly failed on Crete: "At one time, the whole operation was within a hair's breadth of disaster because the airheads, which were too weak and too far apart, were being whittled down."

The Kriegsmarine's (German Navy's) Admiral Schüster was responsible for landing reinforcements of troops and heavy equipment by sea, but had no German naval units under his command for his task. His transport vessels were small caiques that had been captured during the Greek campaign and were assembled in the port of Piraeus.

The final plan

The attack plan finally adopted by Göring was a compromise solution: 10,000 troops were to be dropped by parachute, 750 transported by glider, 5000 air-landed in aircraft and 7000 brought in by sea. The first wave had two objectives. First, men of the 1st, 2nd 3rd and 4th Battalions of the Luftlande-Sturmregiment would land at Maleme airfield in gliders and by parachute. Second, the 3rd Parachute Regiment would drop near Canea, the capital of Crete, and take it, and also seize the port of Suda.

Below: *Mountain troops wait to be airlifted to Crete. During the early hours of 21 May, the Fallschirmjäger secured Hill 107, and a lone Ju 52 was able to land, unload ammunition, load casualties and then take off again. Student's window of opportunity had arrived, and in the afternoon he flew in the 2nd Battalion of the 100th Mountain Regiment. Part of the battalion was used to reinforce paratroopers while the latter reorganised themselves for further attacks, while the others were assigned to the defence of the captured airfield. The remaining two companies of the Luftlande-Sturmregiment were also landed at Maleme on the afternoon of the 21st.*

Above: *German mountain troops on Crete. Ringel's 5th Mountain Division comprised the 85th Gebirgsjäger Regiment, 100th Gebirgsjäger Regiment, 95 Gebirgs Artillery Regiment and the 95th Gebirgs Motorcycle, Pioneer, Antitank and Reconnaissance Battalions. The 5th Mountain Division was slowly flown into Maleme, and began to tilt the balance in favour of the Germans, especially after a British counterattack against the airfield failed in the early hours of 22 May. By 24 May the Germans were able to land supplies at Maleme unmolested, the British having pulled back farther east. The battle now moved into its second phase: the struggle for Suda Bay.*

The second wave would come in some eight hours later on two other objectives: Fallschirmjäger of the 2nd Parachute Regiment would drop on Retimo and its airfield, and the 1st Parachute Regiment would drop on Heraklion and its airfield.

On the second day, follow-on troops of the 5th Mountain Division would be airlifted to the three airfields (Maleme, Retimo and Heraklion) which had been, hopefully, taken by the first wave. Admiral Schüster's convoys would off-load men and supplies at Heraklion, Suda Bay and other minor ports that had been captured. Throughout the operation the fighters and bombers of VIII Flieger Corps would maintain German air superiority overhead.

The state of the garrison

On the eve of the invasion of Crete, the island garrison consisted of around 27,500 British and Commonwealth troops and 14,000 Greeks, all under the command of Major-General Bernard Freyberg, the commanding general of the 2nd New Zealand Division. The original garrison – 5000 men – was fully equipped, but the troops that had been evacuated from Greece were tired, disorganised and only lightly equipped. The Cretans offered their assistance to the Allies, even though they had suffered from air raids and many of their young men had been taken prisoner during the Greek campaign. The only armour available to the defenders consisted of eight medium and 16 light tanks, plus a

Below: *British shipping under attack in Suda Bay. Though the paratroopers at Heraklion and Retimo were still contained, Freyberg knew that these places were sideshows compared to the struggle for Canea and Suda. If he could hold the latter, reinforcements could still be sent to him. However, on 25 May the Germans attacked. The 85th Gebirgsjäger Regiment assaulted Alikianou to cut the main road south of Suda Bay, the 100th Gebirgsjäger Regiment attacked Galatas, the Maleme paratroopers under Ramcke (who had flown in with 500 paras) attacked in the north, while the 3rd Parachute Regiment struck south of Galatas. The fighting was savage, but the Germans had entered Canea by 27 May and taken control of Suda Bay.*

few light personnel carriers. Allied artillery consisted of captured Italian guns, 10 3.7in howitzers and some antiaircraft batteries.

Despite the defenders' deficiencies, it was obvious to the British High Command that a full-scale invasion of Crete would take place, and so General Freyberg disposed his forces accordingly: to guard against airborne landings on the three airfields at Maleme, Retimo and Heraklion, and seaborne landings in Suda Bay and on adjacent beaches. His main force was assigned to the defence of the vital Maleme airfield. His air cover was woeful, though: 36 aircraft, of which less than half were operational (German preparatory bombing raids damaged the airfields, and the aircraft were withdrawn from the island the day before the invasion began).

The British naval presence in the area was much stronger. The fleet was split into two forces: one consisting of two cruisers and four destroyers, which was detailed to intercept any seaborne invader north of the island; and the other made up of two battleships and eight destroyers, which was to screen the island against a possible intervention by the Italian fleet northwest of Crete. Decoding of German Enigma traffic meant the British were aware of German plans to invade Crete, but they believed an airborne invasion could not succeed without

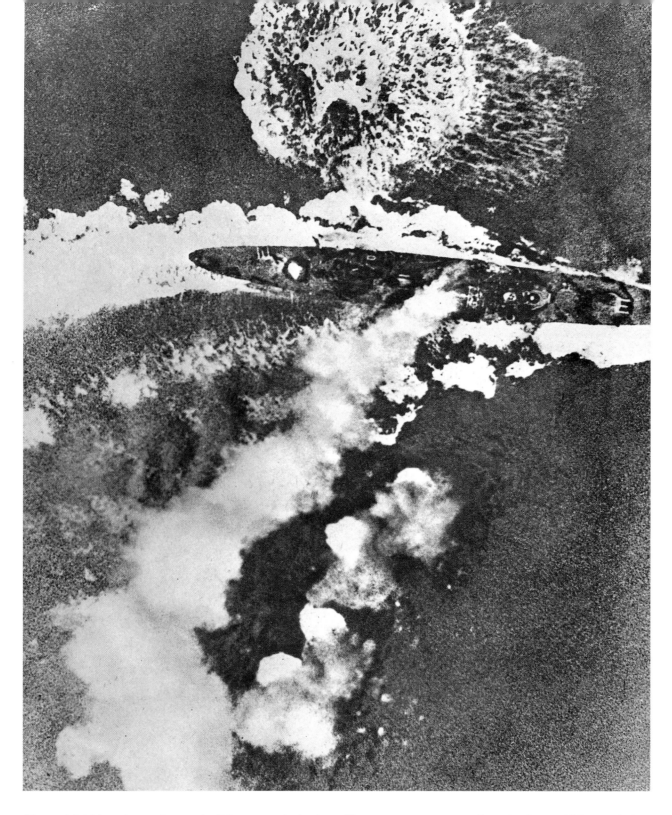

Above: *A British cruiser under attack off Crete. Despite German aerial superiority, the seaborne invasion was stopped when the first convoy was intercepted by a British naval task force which was on its way to Suda to land reinforcements and supplies. The Royal Navy sank most of the convoy, drowning many German troops. A second convoy was recalled to save it from a similar fate.*

the landing of heavy weapons, troops and supplies by sea. If the Royal Navy could intercept these reinforcements, therefore, the battle would be won.

Preceded by large-scale dive-bombing attacks, the invasion began on 20 May 1941. At Maleme, elements of the Sturmregiment's 1st Battalion landed their DFS 230 gliders west and south of the airfield at 07:15 hours. The 3rd Battalion became badly dispersed and dropped into the middle of New Zealand defenders, where they were destroyed in a matter of minutes. The 4th Battalion dropped without too much difficulty just west of Tavronitis, while the 2nd Battalion dropped as planned into the area east of the Spilia and encountered no opposition. A reinforcement platoon that dropped farther west near Kastelli was annihilated by Greek troops and armed civilians.

Generalmajor Meindl had parachuted in with his regimental staff in the 4th Battalion's sector at 07:15 hours, but he was seriously wounded when he was shot through the chest and so command of the regiment was passed on to Major Stentzler, commander of the 2nd Battalion.

A gliderborne assault by Kampfgruppe (Battle Group) *Altmann* (the 1st and 2nd Companies of the Sturmregiment) landed to secure vital objectives near Canea, but suffered heavy casualties. Hauptmann Gustav Altmann was captured on Crete on 22 May and was held in captivity throughout the rest of the war. The 3rd Parachute Regiment was dropped to the southwest of Canea, and many men were killed by New Zealanders. In the face of heavy fighting the paras succeeded in securing Agia, and the prison there was used as a headquarters for Oberst Richard Heidrich and his regimental staff, who had dropped to the southwest of the village (at this time Generalleutnant Wilhelm Süssmann, who was to meet up with the staff of the 7th Flieger Division, was killed when his glider crashed on the island of Aegina).

Below: *Fallschirmjäger with British prisoners on Crete. By 29 May British forces were withdrawing south to Sfakia, though Ringel at first failed to spot this, and decided to strike east to relieve Retimo and Heraklion. Contact with Retimo was made on the 29th and with Heraklion the next day. The Royal Navy performed superbly during the evacuation, embarking 14,800 men and returning them to Egypt in the face of constant enemy air attack.*

Above: *Student's victorious men stand guard over British prisoners. Hauptmann Freiherr von der Heydte, commander of the 1st Battalion, 3rd Parachute Regiment, summed up the Crete operation thus: "German paratroopers demonstrated that it was possible to carry out an airborne operation on a large scale, in which parachute units were not employed solely in support of ground forces, but on their own in order to solve unique and isolated strategical problems." But the cost had been high: 7000 German soldiers killed or wounded.*

By midday on 20 May, the 3rd Parachute Regiment was unable to reach Canea because of the enemy and was suffering heavy casualties, and the Luftlande-Sturmregiment failed to take Hill 107 (to the south of and overlooking Maleme airfield) and the airfield itself. To compound the crisis, aircraft losses, problems with refuelling the Ju 52s and dust on the Greek airfields affected the timetable of the second wave. This forced the second drop to fly in small groups instead of en masse.

Oberst Alfred Sturm's 2nd Parachute Regiment dropped onto Retimo at 15:00 hours. Widely scattered, the men immediately encountered resistance from the Australian 19th Brigade. Progress was slight. It was a similar story at Heraklion, where the 1st Parachute Regiment met a determined defence and failed to take the airfield. Receiving news about the initial landings, Student decided to try to land the mountain troops at Maleme instead of Heraklion in an effort to save the whole operation.

On 21 May, the Fallschirmjäger were able to take control of the vital Hill 107 due to a mistaken withdrawal by the New Zealanders. This left the way open for the Germans to capture Maleme airfield. German air strikes against New Zealand positions east of the airfield began at 14:30 hours, followed by parachute drops by reserves from the 1st and 2nd Parachute Regiments. These, together with the men already on the ground, managed to overrun the airfield defences. With the airfield still under artillery fire, the first Ju 52 carrying mountain troop reinforcements landed at Maleme at 16:00 hours. Many aircraft collided or were destroyed by enemy artillery fire, but the troops were off-loaded nevertheless.

On 21 May the Royal Navy intercepted the German flotilla transporting troops and supplies. Though many boats managed to escape back to Greece, many others were sent to the bottom of the sea. On a more favourable note for the Germans was a failed British attack on Maleme, which turned out to be the first decisive battle on the island. The commander of the 5th Mountain Division, General Ringel, took command of the units around Maleme and reorganised them. Meanwhile, the paratroopers around Retimo and Heraklion were still fighting to maintain their positions. However, by 23 May the crisis of the campaign had passed, and units of Ringel's force had linked up with the remnants of the 3rd Parachute Regiment near Canea. But the British continued to put up a dogged resistance, especially around the fortified positions of Kastelli and Galatas. Indeed, the battle there lasted for 48 hours and was among the most intense of the whole operation.

On the evening of 25 May, the mountain troops took the British positions at Kastelli and Galatas and two days later the Germans, now receiving reinforcements flown into Maleme, launched an assault against Canea itself. The 1st

Below: *Cretan partisans about to be executed in retaliation for the mutilation of dead and wounded Fallschirmjäger at Maleme. At least 135 paratroopers from the 3rd Battalion, Luftlande-Sturmregiment, were killed by partisans. The village of Kandenos was also wiped out in retaliation for partisan brutalities.*

Battalion of the 3rd Parachute Regiment outflanked the British rearguard positions and entered the town. The same unit took Suda on 28 May, and from that date the battle turned into a chase. The next day Ringel's forces linked up with the parachute units at Retimo and Heraklion, which had been badly mauled in the campaign. British forces were now retreating south to be taken off the island by the Royal Navy, Freyberg having been authorised to evacuate on the 27th.

Mopping up

The Germans now controlled the whole of the north coast, and detachments of the mountain division were pushing forward to prevent the evacuation. The last battle in Crete was fought near the village of Sfakia, where the British rearguards fought to keep the Germans away from the evacuation beachhead. By 1 June the campaign was over and the island was in German hands. The price of victory had been high: one in four of the paratroopers dropped on the island had been killed, with many more wounded.

Von Der Heydte later gave one reason for the losses suffered by the Fallschirmjäger: "the lack of tactical experience of the German paratroopers – particularly of their junior officers – must be mentioned. Courage, enthusiasm and devotion cannot make up for lack of experience and training." Student himself commented that Crete was "the grave of the German Paratroopers". Hitler was shocked at the losses incurred in taking Crete, and a combined German-Italian airborne assault to capture Malta, which was much smaller and more lightly defended, in 1942 was cancelled on his orders: "The affair will go wrong and will cost too many lives." In effect the Fallschirmjäger had been grounded on Hitler's orders – there would be no more large-scale airborne operations in the war. From now on the paratroopers would fight as infantry, first in Africa and then in Europe, but would do so brilliantly.

Above: *The Kreta cuff title. It takes the form of a white cotton strip with a border of yellow cotton. In between the borders, in capital letters, is embroidered KRETA in yellow cotton. Either side of the title is a sprig of acanthus leaves in a stylised pattern. Some reference works have only recognised a band made of off-white cotton. However, there is a variation of this strip produced in an off-white felt strip. The Fallschirmjäger criterion for the award was to have been engaged in a glider or parachute landing between 20 and 27 May 1941 on the island of Crete.*

Right: *The Fallschirmjäger won no less than 23 Knight's Crosses for their heroism on Crete. Göring himself issued an Order of the Day on 2 June 1941, acknowledging their feats on the island: "Paratroopers: filled with an unstoppable offensive spirit, you have entirely on your own defeated the numerically superior enemy in an heroic, bitter struggle."*

Above: *A German general described the Fallschirmjäger on the Eastern Front thus: "Superior in their discipline, toughness and training, with an exemplary spirit of cooperation."*

RUSSIA –
A FORCE BLED WHITE

On the Eastern Front the Fallschirmjäger fought as infantry, but soon earned a reputation for courage and steadfastness in a series of vicious and unrelenting battles against the Red Army. But the parachute divisions were to discover to their cost that courage and audacity are no substitute for superior armoured and artillery firepower.

Left: *A Fallschirm-jäger motorcyclist steers his machine through the Russian mud. The 7th Flieger Division was sent to the Eastern Front at the end of September 1941, just in time for the wet season that began in October, bringing with it the glutinous mud that inhibited movement.*

The usual reason given for the lack of any large-scale airborne operations after the Battle of Crete in 1941 was that Hitler, horrified at the losses incurred, would not sanction risky airborne missions. While this is true, a post-war study on German airborne operations commissioned by the US Army provides another reason. The contributors to the study included von der Heydte, Kesselring, Meindl and Student, and their comments are pertinent: "The airborne operation against Crete resulted in very serious losses … The parachute troops were particularly affected. Since everything Germany possessed in the way of parachute troops had been committed in the attack on Crete and had been reduced in that campaign to about one-third of their original strength, too few qualified troops remained to carry out large-scale airborne operations at the beginning of the Russian campaign. Air transportation was also insufficient for future operations." Thus when Operation "Barbarossa", the German invasion of the Soviet Union, opened on 22 June 1941, the 7th

Flieger Division was back at its bases in Germany for rest and refitting after the losses suffered on Crete.

The German advance in Russia slowed at the end of September 1941, as Army Groups North, Centre and South ground to a halt in the mud and against stiff Soviet resistance, and units of the division were mobilised for service in the East. The 1st and 3rd Battalions of the 1st Parachute Regiment and the 2nd Battalion of the Luftlande-Sturmregiment (Airlanding Assault Regiment) were sent to the Leningrad area to fight with Army Group North's Eighteenth Army.

The Fallschirmjäger were deployed to the east of the city on the River Neva, where Red Army troops of the Volkhov Front were pushing west to relieve Leningrad. The fighting on the Neva in October 1941 was bitter, but the paratroopers managed to hold off the Soviet attacks. The 7th Flieger Division's headquarters arrived at the front in mid-October, and the Parachute Engineer Battalion shortly after. The latter went straight into action in woods on the west

Left: *Sentry duty beside a Russian railway track. This photograph shows the Fallschirmjäger field-grey woollen cloth trousers, which had two side pockets, two hip pockets, two leg openings set into the outer seams just above knee level and a single fob pocket. They had a "V" section cut into the outer side of the cuff, with two lengths of tape sewn into each side of these sections. This meant the bottom of each trouser leg could be gathered and tied around the ankle of the boot to give a baggy appearance (paratrooper trousers were designed to allow individuals to reach inside the legs and unfasten and withdraw their knee protectors). The opening let into the outer seam of the right leg had three concealed internal press-stud fasteners, while the leg pocket had an external wedge-shaped flap sewn into the leg seam and secured by another two press-studs (as can be seen). The paratrooper's so-called "gravity knife", which was designed to enable individuals to cut their way out of a parachute harness after a bad landing, was housed in this pocket. As its name suggests, the blade was activated by gravity: a spring-pressure lever freed the blade.*

Above: *A motorcycle team dismounts to deal with enemy troops or partisans in northern Russia. Between September and December 1941, the following Fallschirmjäger formations were deployed to the Leningrad area of operations: Headquarters, 1st and 3rd Battalions, 1st Parachute Regiment; Headquarters, 1st, 2nd and 3rd Battalions, 3rd Parachute Regiment; 1st and 2nd Companies, Parachute Engineer Battalion; 1st and 3rd Companies, 7th Parachute Artillery Battalion; 1st Company, 7th Parachute Medical Battalion; 2nd Company, 7th Parachute Antitank Battalion; 2nd Company, 7th Parachute Machine Gun Battalion; and 2nd Battalion, Airlanding Assault Regiment.*

side of the Neva. For the next two months the Red Army battered the Fallschirmjäger, to no avail. In December 1941, the Fallschirmjäger in the Leningrad area were pulled out of the line and sent back to Germany for rest.

The 2nd Parachute Regiment, a battalion of the Assault Regiment and units of the Antitank and Machine Gun Battalions were sent to the Ukraine to bolster Army Group South. This force – Kampfgruppe *Sturm*, commanded by Oberst Alfred Sturm – defended a sector along the River Mius around the town of Charzysk throughout the winter of 1941 and into early 1942. During this period the Russians and the weather inflicted heavy casualties on the paras.

Battles of attrition

The new year witnessed a number of Soviet offensives, against which the paratroopers showed their true worth. As élite troops they were ideally suited to holding ground in the face of overwhelming odds, as they had displayed on Crete. This certainly endeared them to Hitler, who was obsessed with not yielding an inch of territory. Kampfgruppe *Sturm* held all Soviet assaults, and Kampfgruppe *Meindl* (formed from the Assault Regiment's 1st Battalion, units of the Artillery Regiment and the Regimental Headquarters) was rushed south to reinforce Sturm's men. A series of battles developed in the Yuknov sector which lasted for weeks, with the paras holding back the Soviets and inflicting heavy casualties on the attackers. Once the attacks abated, Kampfgruppe *Meindl* was sent north to an area around the River Volkhov, southeast of Leningrad. In March 1942, the 2nd Parachute Regiment was also moved to the Volkhov Front, being placed under the command of the 21st Infantry Division.

The Soviet forces of the Volkhov and Northwest Fronts launched a massive offensive east of Leningrad to try to break the siege on 8 May. The 2nd

Left: *Clearing a Red Army bunker on the Neva Front with a Flammenwerfer (Flamethrower). This particular model is the Flammenwerfer 41, with its two horizontal cylindrical tanks on a backpack frame. At first a battery-initiated hydrogen ignition system was used, but following service on the Eastern Front, where it was discovered to be unreliable in very cold conditions, the igniter was changed to a cartridge-based method. In this system a fresh pyrotechnic cartridge ignited the fuel as it left the projector nozzle every time the projector trigger was depressed. The fuel capacity was seven litres (1.5 gallons), which gave between five and six blasts, each one lasting between two and three seconds and shooting a jet of flame out to a range of 25m (83ft).*

Below: *On fatigues near Leningrad. Elements of the 2nd Parachute Regiment, Airlanding Assault Regiment and 7th Parachute Machine Gun Battalion were also deployed to the Moscow sector of the front in 1941.*

Above: *Fallschirmjäger on the Eastern Front kitted out in white cotton covers. These could be worn over all the uniform and equipment and could be easily washed and cleaned by laundry units immediately behind the front. Note the white helmets. For use in snow conditions individuals painted their helmets with a thick coating of whitewash. This was preferred to white paint because when the spring came and the snows disappeared the white could be washed off with water. Armament consists of a mixture of rifles and submachine guns.*

Right: *Surveying enemy positions from a slit trench on the Leningrad front. Obergefreiter Maue, a member of the Parachute Airlanding Assault Regiment, provides an insight into the nature of the fighting during the first phase of the Fallschirmjäger campaign on the Eastern Front: "Advancing in the sector was made even more difficult by the bunkers the Russians had built to defend it, even though the Neva was within reach. During my stint at the front, I could clearly see the suburbs of the city of Leningrad."*

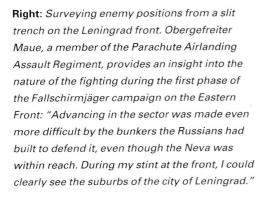

Parachute Regiment, located in and around the small town of Lipovka, put up a desperate resistance and threw back waves of Soviet tanks and infantry. The paras held, but were so depleted that in July they were back in Germany for some well-earned rest.

In the summer of 1942 the majority of the 7th Flieger Division was resting and refitting in Normandy, where a 4th Parachute Regiment was added to its order of battle to make up for the transfer of the 2nd Parachute Regiment to North Africa. This unit was commanded by Oberst Erich Walther.

During this period OKW devised a plan for an airdrop in southern Russia to capture a number of oil fields. This operation was cancelled in September, though, and the 7th Flieger Division was allocated to Army Group Centre. The division moved into positions near Smolensk, being tasked with defending a 90km (56-mile) sector north of the Smolensk-Vitebsk highway. The winter was fairly quiet, as the Wehrmacht and Red Army were locked in combat in and around Stalingrad farther south. The lull lasted until March 1943.

Expansion of the airborne arm

At the end of the month the Soviets opened their offensive against the positions held by the 7th Flieger Division. Massive artillery barrages and infantry and tank attacks failed to overrun the Fallschirmjäger. Generalmajor Richard Heidrich was allowed to pull his men out of the line once the attacks had petered out. Transferred to southern France, it was joined by the newly raised 2nd Parachute Division, and both divisions were grouped under XI Flieger

Above: *A well-wrapped paratrooper ski patrol in Russia. Note the fur caps sporting Luftwaffe eagles worn by the two soldiers on the left. Luftwaffe troops fighting as infantry on the Eastern Front were first issued with reversible winter clothing during the winter of 1942–43. Some of these men are wearing standard-issue toques around their necks. Wool-knitted toques were essential items on the Eastern Front. There are recorded instances of soldiers not wearing toques removing their helmets in sub-zero conditions to find that the tops of their ears had come away – frozen to the helmet lining! The icy conditions of the Russian winter made metal brittle and often snapped slender firing pins. Even machine guns could seize in the sub-zero temperatures. Thus in battles with Red Army infantry German troops often fought with knives, bayonets and entrenching tools to defend their positions.*

Left: *A winter training exercise in Russia. The paratrooper on the right is in the process of throwing a Stielgranate (Stick Grenade). The wooden handle acted as a throwing aid, giving the weapon a greater range than egg-shaped grenades. Before throwing, the user removed a screw cap over the base of the throwing handle, grasped a bead on the end of the double length of cord which ran through the length of the throwing handle, and pulled it. This set off the detonator time delay, allowing the grenade to be thrown at once. After four and a half seconds the warhead exploded, producing blast and a small amount of fragmentation. The Luftwaffe took delivery of 3,740,200 stick grenades during 1943–44 alone.*

Corps. The 7th Flieger Division now became the 1st Parachute Division. All other para units fighting on the Eastern Front had been withdrawn for refitting by July 1943, but the worsening situation in Russia meant that it would not be long before they were again sent east.

Away from the front there was a major expansion of the German airborne arm in 1943. As well as the two divisions mentioned above, the 3rd Parachute Division was formed in October 1943 and the 4th Parachute Division was created in November 1943. The new divisions were needed: by end of the year the Germans had lost the Battle of Kursk and the strategic initiative in the East.

In early November 1943, the 2nd Parachute Division was ordered to the Eastern Front to take up positions near the Russian-held town of Zhitomir. Arriving between 17–27 November 1943 under the command of Generalleutnant Gustav Wilke, it was placed under the command of XXXXII

Below: *A 28mm SPbz 41 (Schwere Panzerbusche – heavy antitank rifle – 41) in action with Fallschirmjäger personnel. Though small in calibre, it was an excellent light antitank weapon which was simple to operate and required only a two-man crew. This photograph shows the light version designed for airborne use, with small wheels and a lightened carriage.*

Above: A break from combat on an airfield away from the front behind German lines. Between November 1941 and March 1942, the first winter on the Eastern Front, the following paratrooper units saw service in Russia, in the Stalino sector: 1st and 2nd Battalions, 2nd Parachute Regiment; 4th Battalion, Airlanding Assault Regiment; 1st Company, 7th Parachute Antitank Battalion; 2nd and 3rd Companies, 7th Parachute Medical Battalion; and the 7th Parachute Machine Gun Battalion.

Left: Another of the seemingly endless snow patrols. The lead paratrooper appears to be armed with the Kar 98a bolt-action rifle, a carbine version of the weapon, which was designed for cavalry use. It was actually only marginally smaller than the Gew 98: 1.1m (3.67ft) instead of 1.25m (4.2ft). Mauser produced a special Fallschirmjäger version of its Kar 98K, which could be divided into two parts by means of a threaded junction. However, submachine guns became more available to airborne troops as the war progressed, and their compact dimensions and firepower made them more attractive than bolt-action rifles.

Left: *An Oberleutnant (Flying Officer) on the Eastern Front during the winter of 1942–43. He is wearing padded winter reversible trousers over his green jump smock, while he carries six spare 32-round 9mm box magazines for his MP 40 submachine gun in the whitened pouches. During this period the 7th Flieger Division was active in the Smolensk area, though only in small-scale actions.*

Below: *A Pak crew of the 7th Parachute Antitank Battalion in the Smolensk area in early 1943. The battalion's 3rd Company served on the Eastern Front from October 1942 to 6 April 1943, while the 5th and 6th Companies were also deployed to Russia in October 1942.*

Left: *A Marder II self-propelled gun in Fallschirmjäger service on the Eastern Front. Late in the war, in January 1945, the airborne arm formed a number of Fallschirm-Panzer-Jagd-Bataillone (Parachute Tank Hunter Battalions). These were Nos 51, 52, 43 and 54, and all four were formed on 29 January.*

Corps and deployed east of Zhitomir. The Red Army aim was to take Kiev, destroy the Fourth Panzer Army, seize communications centres west of the Dnieper, including Zhitomir, and eventually annihilate the entire German southern wing. By December the Red Army had massed a large force northeast of the city to breach the German defences and reach the Dniester, though German units managed to plug the gaps created by the Soviet advance. On 15 December the 2nd Parachute Division was airlifted to Kirovograd and put into the line at Klinzy. It was supported by the 11th Panzer Division and the 286th Self-Propelled Brigade.

Below: *The same vehicle photographed from a different angle. The Marder II was armed with a 75mm Pak 40/2 gun and one MG 34 machine gun. Manned by a crew of three, this particular vehicle has five "kills" to its credit judging by the rings around the barrel of its gun.*

Above: *Training to deal with enemy tanks on the Eastern Front (note the shadows of the cameraman and his assistant in the foreground). This tank appears to be a BT-7, which was the main Soviet type in service in 1939–41, though by the end of 1941 the Germans had encountered the more potent T-34 in ever-increasing numbers. Armed with only light antitank weapons and grenades, Fallschirmjäger personnel were often required to get close to enemy tanks to knock them out. Individuals never lacked for courage, but such tactics nearly always resulted in heavy casualties.*

Fierce fighting developed around Novgorodka and the surrounding hills. By 23 December the division had stabilised the line, but had taken many casualties.

In early January 1944 the Red Army renewed its offensive against the 2nd Parachute Division, and numbers began to tell. The 2nd Battalion of 5th Regiment was destroyed, and by 6 January the 7th, 5th and 2nd Regiments had been forced to pull out of the Novgorodka area due to Red Army pressure. Taking up positions near Kirovograd, the paras dug in and waited for the next attack. It came in March, when Russian forces near Kiev struck south towards the 2nd Parachute Division's positions. By the last week of March the Fallschirmjäger had been forced across the River Bug where they set up defensive positions on the opposite bank. Being pushed back all the time, by May they were on the River Dniester. They had been decimated in the fighting, and so at the end of the month the division was transferred to Germany for rest and

Right: *The strain of service is clearly etched on the face of this paratrooper. By the end of 1943 the German Army was on the strategic defensive in the East, and parachute divisions were being rushed from one crisis to another. In November 1943, for example, the 2nd Parachute Division was trying to halt the Soviet advance around Zhitomir, while in December it was airlifted to Kirovograd to push back Red Army units threatening the line.*

Below: *Of interest in this photograph is the Haft-Holladung 3kg (6.6lb) magnetic antitank charge on the left side of the figure on the left. Used by infantry close-quarter tank-killer units, it had three strong magnets to allow it to be placed on an enemy tank. It could penetrate up to 140mm (5.5in) of armour, though it required nerves of steel to fix on a target.*

Above: *Fallschirmjäger with Soviet prisoners. In general, paratrooper units did not show callousness towards captured foes in Russia, certainly not like that displayed by the more ideologically indoctrinated and motivated Waffen-SS. In Tunisia in November 1942, for example, troops of the 5th Parachute Regiment treated captured British paras well, and their commander, Oberstleutnant Walter Koch, prevented them from being executed by other Axis soldiers. That said, Fallschirmjäger did carry out reprisals against civilians when ordered to do so.*

Right: *Time for a brief smoke during a lull in the fighting. In the combat around Kirovograd in December 1943 and January 1944, the 2nd Parachute Division was bled white trying to halt the Red Army advance. The 5th Parachute Regiment's 2nd Battalion was all but wiped out, and the 7th, 5th and 2nd Parachute Regiments were badly mauled. Savage fighting in this sector erupted again in March, and over two months of continuous combat followed, during which the division was pushed back west. Totally shattered, by the end of May it was back in Germany for rest and refitting – it would never again serve on the Eastern Front.*

refitting. It was the last time that the 2nd Parachute Division would see action on the Eastern Front.

The only other paratrooper unit to see action in 1944 was the 21st Parachute Pioneer Battalion under the command of Major Rudolf Witzig of Eben Emael fame. In mid-1944 Army Group Centre had been shattered by the Red Army's Operation "Bagration", and by July the Soviets were approaching the Baltic. On 25 July 1944, Witzig's engineers were positioned on the road between Dunaburg and Kovno in Lithuania. The Soviet tanks, supported by infantry and artillery, attacked the next day. Despite fighting heroically the engineers were soon encircled, and Witzig was forced to retreat to the main German lines. Witzig's battalion stayed on the Eastern Front until October 1944, but by then it had been decimated by combat and was disbanded, the survivors being sent to other parachute units.

By the beginning of 1945 the Red Army was about to commence the final operations that would bring about victory on the Eastern Front. The Wehrmacht scraped together its last reserves for this final campaign, but at this stage of the war many units were very depleted both in personnel and equipment. The newly raised

Above: *As the war progressed, especially on the Eastern Front where Fallschirmjäger units were used as conventional infantry, varying methods of camouflaging the steel helmet were employed. This could be either on an individual or unit basis. Unofficial helmet coverings used by paratroopers included netting, wire and painted camouflage patterns.*

9th and 10th Parachute Divisions, for example, were both understrength. The 9th was deployed outside Stettin on the Baltic, and in April it was containing a Russian bridgehead on the west bank of the River Oder. On the 16th the 9th was subjected to an intense artillery barrage, and from then on its units began to disintegrate. The 2nd Battalion, 27th Regiment, and the 3rd Battalion, 26th Regiment, were wiped out. The rest of the division pulled back, but was then overpowered by Soviet tanks.

By late April 1945 the Red Army had surrounded Berlin itself. What was left of the 9th Parachute Division withdrew to the central district of the city to defend the Führerbunker and surrounding ministry buildings. When the city surrendered the remnants of the division went into Soviet captivity.

The 10th Parachute Division was sent to southern Austria to contain a developing crisis early in April 1945: Soviet forces were flooding through Hungary, and Army Group South desperately needed reinforcements. On 3 April advance units of the division reached Graz. Digging in around the town of Feldbach, the paras held off T-34 tanks with infantry antitank weapons and 88mm guns. However, losses were high and the Artillery Battalion was all but destroyed.

On 27 April, the 10th Parachute Division was pulled out of the line (though the 30th Regiment remained in the Danube Valley) and transported by railway to Bruenn in the Sudetenland to join what was left of the Eighteenth Army. The remnants of the 10th Parachute Division made their last stand to the north of Bruenn, where they were wiped out. The 30th Regiment managed to surrender to US forces, but was subsequently handed over to the Russians. The Fallschirmjäger war on the Eastern Front was over.

Below: *A Pak crew in blizzard conditions waits for a target to appear. Many Fallschirmjäger units became expert at knocking out tanks on the Eastern Front. Major Rudolf Witzig, commander of the 21st Parachute Pioneer Regiment, and his unit were mentioned in Wehrmacht despatches on 8 August 1944 after destroying 27 Soviet tanks in a single engagement near Kumele in Lithuania. On this occasion antitank guns were not used: the paratroopers knocked out the tanks with satchel charges and magnetic mines.*

Left: *As well as the Flammenwerfer 41 (shown here), the Fallschirmjäger received the one-shot Einstossflammenwerfer 46 flamethrower. First used in 1944, it was intended as an airborne close-quarter weapon. It held enough fuel to project a single half-second blast to a range of 27m (90ft). However, by this time there was no pressing need for airborne weapons.*

Below: *Hitching a ride west as 1944 draws to a close. Despite the crumbling of the Eastern Front in late 1944 and early 1945, the morale and fighting ability of the Fallschirmjäger divisions in the East remained high. Notwithstanding fierce combat, on 8 April 1945 the 9th Parachute Division still had a strength of 11,600 men, while the 10th Parachute Division could muster 10,700 men on 17 April.*

Above: *Luftwaffe reversible winter heavy duty, double-breasted over-jackets and over-trousers were very comfortable – hence, perhaps, the smiles on the faces of these Fallschirmjäger on the Eastern Front.*

Right: *Typical Fallschirmjäger appearance during the last winter of the war on the Eastern Front – dirty reversible winter uniform, MG 42 machine gun slung over the shoulder and a belt of 7.92mm ammunition round the neck. Stick grenades were often tucked into the belt.*

Above: *An overloaded motorcycle and sidecar in Tunisia in mid-1943. Note the Oberleutnant (Flying Officer) with his two wings and rectangular bar on his left sleeve.*

NORTH AFRICA

Though the Fallschirmjäger contribution to the war in North Africa was small, during the later part of the campaign in Tunisia paratrooper units had an influence out of all proportion to their size in staving off defeat in the face of heavy odds. When the Axis war effort in North Africa collapsed in May 1943, many paratroopers were left behind and entered captivity.

Left: *A Fallschirmjäger sentry on duty in North Africa, dressed in Luftwaffe tropical clothing. The German Air Force termed the colour of its tropical clothing Khakibrun, though it was actually light tan. His bandolier is blue-grey in colour, and his helmet cover is in splinter camouflage.*

Because Hitler had lost confidence in large-scale airborne operations after the fall of Crete, Operation "Hercules", the planned assault on the island of Malta, never took place. One reason for this was that the operation would have been prepared and launched from Italy, and by 1942 the Führer had little confidence in the quality of Italian troops. In addition, he was convinced that the enemy would get to know of the operation beforehand, therefore destroying the element of surprise.

Despite the High Command's misgivings about "Hercules", the airborne arm was confident about the operation and had even organised a unit for the Malta operation. The so-called *Ramcke* Parachute Brigade, under the command of Generalmajor Bernhard Hermann Ramcke, consisted of Battalion *Kroh* (formed from the 1st Battalion of the 2nd Parachute Regiment), Battalion *Hübner* (formed from the 2nd Battalion of the 5th Parachute Regiment), Battalion *Burckhardt* (formed from a demonstration battalion), the newly raised

Battalion *von der Heydte*, an Artillery Battalion (formed from the 2nd Battalion of the 7th Flieger Division's artillery regiment), Antitank Company, Signals Company and Pioneer Company. Training continued apace, and the paratroopers started to receive new airborne equipment. First, there was a 48mm antitank gun with a tapered bore that fired a solid projectile. However, though it was a marked improvement on the 37mm model, it proved to be ineffective against British tanks in North Africa and production was discontinued in 1943. Far more useful was the Panzerwurfmine (magnetic antitank mine), which was introduced as a special weapon for fighting tanks at close ranges, though it was soon superseded by the Panzerfaust antitank grenade launcher. For the Malta operation the firm of Siemens-Halske developed a portable radio set that could be easily carried by one man. It had a range of 288km (180 miles) and a battery life of six hours.

Deployment to North Africa

But the drop on Malta never took place, and instead in July 1942 the *Ramcke* Parachute Brigade was sent to bolster the Axis war effort in North Africa. At this time Field Marshal Rommel was at the height of his success, having smashed the British Eighth Army's armour at the Battle of Gazala (28 May–13 June) and taken the port of Tobruk (21 June). He had then invaded Egypt and forced the British back to the Alamein gap, but had there been held in July. And such were his logistical problems that he needed to defeat the Eighth Army decisively to prevent the collapse of his Afrika Corps.

Tobruk had been a disappointment, being able to handle only 610 tonnes (600 tons) a day. Moreover, British bombing raids in early August reduced its capacity still further, and British naval and air units intercepted and destroyed thousands of tons of Axis military cargo before they reached port. From 1–20

Above: *Generalmajor Bernhard Hermann Ramcke (far left), commander of the* Ramcke Parachute Brigade. *His unit was effectively abandoned after the Battle of El Alamein in October 1942, because it lacked motor transport. However, Ramcke and his men were determined to escape west to link up with Rommel's retreating forces. Capturing a British transport column, it made contact with the Afrika Corps on 7 November. Colonel Hans von Luck, a panzer commander under Rommel, recorded the event: "General Ramcke was brought to us in a scout car. He looked emaciated and asked to be taken, at once, to Rommel. His paratroopers – an élite unit – had been through an adventurous time. I shall never forget the sight of Ramcke's men coming towards us, exhausted, out of the desert. For reasons of space, they had left everything behind except for weapons and water, but their morale was astonishing." The brigade's strength, originally 4000 men, had dwindled to a mere 600.*

Left: *A member of the* Ramcke *Brigade in Egypt in September 1942. The brigade was made up of four battle groups: Battalion* Kroh *(1st Battalion, 2nd Parachute Regiment); Battalion* von der Heydte *(1st Battalion, 3rd Parachute Regiment); Battalion* Hübner *(2nd Battalion, 5th Parachute Regiment); Battalion* Burckhardt *(XI Flieger Corps' Parachute Training Regiment); and support units. The paratroopers found service in the heat arduous, and there were soon complaints to the High Command about inadequate water rations, scant diet and poor medical care.*

August, Axis forces used twice as many supplies as successfully arrived in North Africa. This meant that German units alone were understrength by 16,000 troops, 210 tanks and around 1600 other vehicles by the end of September. The men of the *Ramcke* Brigade were some of the 24,000 troops and 11,000 Luftwaffe personnel airlifted to North Africa in Ju 52s during July and August, but these men could not be supplied with heavy weapons, artillery, troop carriers, tanks or ammunition. In fact, they imposed a greater strain on already overstretched essential items.

For the Eighth Army, under the command of Lieutenant-General Bernard Montgomery, the reverse was true. During August it received 386 tanks, 446 artillery pieces, 6600 vehicles and 73,200 tonnes (72,000 tons) of supplies. Rommel was placed in an uncomfortable position: he could await the British

Below: *British forces in pursuit of the Afrika Corps after El Alamein, November 1942. Though the* Ramcke *Brigade managed to escape entrapment, the men were pushed to the limits of their endurance. Many succumbed to heatstroke, malaria and dysentery, and a number of Fallschirmjäger had to be sent back to Germany to recuperate.*

attack with all its overwhelming superiority, or he could forestall it by striking as soon as possible (his "window of opportunity" would exist until September, when the balance of forces would be so heavily weighed against him that his chances of mounting an offensive would be gone).

His plan was to launch a feint attack in the centre while his armour would outflank British positions to the south, after which Axis forces would wheel north and head for the sea, encircling enemy forces in the El Alamein position. An integral part of the operation involved the *Ramcke* Brigade, which, together with the Italian Folgore Parachute Division, was to capture the bridges over the Nile at Alexandria and Cairo.

Rommel's attempt to break through at El Alamein resulted in the Battle of Alam Halfa (31 August–7 September), where his tanks were defeated by a combination of fuel shortages and the tactics of the Eighth Army's new commander.

Above: *Wounded Fallschirmjäger in Tunisia. Following the Anglo-American landings in North Africa in November 1942, the Germans started pouring forces into Tunisia. These included elements of the 5th Parachute Regiment under Major Walter Koch and the 11th Parachute Pioneer Battalion under Major Rudolf Witzig. Koch had been named commander of the 5th Parachute Regiment on 11 March 1942, and had been promoted to Oberstleutnant on 20 April.*

Left: *Bernhard Ramcke decorates a Fallschirmjäger NCO in Tunisia. Both men are wearing tropical uniform, the NCO sporting the long-sleeved shirt. Luftwaffe orders issued on 14 February 1942 had laid down what was to be issued to Luftwaffe and Fallschirmjäger troops in tropical areas: one tropical peaked cap with neck protector, one tropical tunic, one pair of long tropical trousers, one pair of tropical shorts, two tropical shirts with long sleeves, two tropical shirts with long sleeves, three tropical vests, three pairs of tropical underpants, two tropical ties, two neck sweat bands, and one pair of lace-up boots.*

There was no parachute drop on the Nile, and German Fallschirmjäger took no part in the action.

In late October the *Ramcke* Brigade was part of the Afrika Corps commanded by General Hans Stumme (Rommel, ill, had flown back to Germany), and was deployed on the Axis right to meet the coming British offensive. It came on the 23rd, when 1000 guns opened the 2nd Battle of El Alamein. Though Axis forces fought with skill and determination, Montgomery's superiority in tanks and men, plus the acute Axis shortage of fuel, began to wear down Italian and German armoured strength. By 2 November, for example, only 35 German tanks remained in action. With his fuel nearly spent and most of his tanks and artillery knocked out, Rommel, having flown back from Europe, decided to retreat. He had started the battle with 104,000 men, 500 tanks and 1200 guns. At the end of the battle he had lost 59,000 men killed, wounded or captured, almost all of his tanks and 400 guns. Ramcke's men had been involved in heavy fighting during the battle, but once the order to withdraw was given the brigade was effectively abandoned. Indeed, all those Axis infantry who had no transport were quickly overrun by the Eighth Army. The *Ramcke* Brigade had no organic transport, but rather than surrender its commander decided to break out to the west. The breakout cost him 450 men alone, but in the process the brigade captured a British supply column which provided it with trucks and supplies. It was an amazing piece of good luck, and enabled

Below: *A member of a Fallschirmjäger Field Police unit checks papers in Tunisia. Round his neck he wears the army pattern duty gorget which displays the army pattern eagle. The half-moon plate and the chain links have a matt-silver finish, while the raised scroll is painted a dark field-grey. The lettering on the scroll, the eagle and the swastika emblems and the pebble-surfaced bosses have a luminous paint finish. The word on the gorget is "Feldgendarmerie", meaning Field Police. Military police operated in each German army's rear areas or in Nazi zones of occupation.*

600 men of the *Ramcke* Brigade to rejoin the Afrika Corps, though not before an arduous trip across the desert.

The Allied Operation "Torch" landings commenced on 8 November 1942, designed to seize Morocco, Algeria and Tunisia as bases for further operations against the Axis alliance. In response, Hitler began sending German troops by air into Tunisia (1000 men per day would arrive between 17 November and the end of December). Although the amount was relatively small, it was enough to check the leading troops of the Allied First Army when they reached the immediate approach to Tunis two-and-a-half weeks after the amphibious landings. The result was a five-month deadlock in the mountainous region covering Bizerta and Tunis.

A small part of these reinforcements were the 1st and 3rd Battalions of the 5th Parachute Regiment under the command of Oberstleutnant Walter Koch, the hero of Eben Emael. They were flown into Tunis to protect its airfields and

Above: *Somewhat apprehensive faces on board a Ju 52 in the Mediterranean theatre. Their concern is understandable: during the first three months of 1943 the Allied air forces in North Africa were receiving large quantities of aircraft and were increasing in strength. Attacks on Luftwaffe transport aircraft were increasing, resulting in mounting losses. The defensive armament carried by a Ju 52 was totally inadequate to stave off enemy fighters: one 13mm and two 7.92mm machine guns.*

Left: *Ju 52s fly into Tunisia in early 1943. Erwin Bauer was a member of the 5th Parachute Regiment and flew in one such airlift: "We were issued with tropical uniforms and then packed our parachutes ... In September or October [1942], the unit was flown to Tunis in a group of 70 Junkers." Another Fallschirmjäger who served in North Africa, Jäger Bohn, gives an insight into the growing Allied air power at this time: "We had hardly set foot in Tunisia when we were bombed by British aircraft."*

take up defensive positions to the west and south of the city. Koch, however, fell ill in Tunisia and had to be ferried back to a German hospital. The 5th Parachute Regiment was closely followed by the 11th Parachute Pioneer Battalion under the command of Major Rudolf Witzig. This unit was an airborne light engineering battalion composed of three field companies (each of three platoons and a machine-gun section) and a signals platoon. First raised in 1942, its strength on arrival in Africa was 716 men. It was used to bolster the Axis defences to the west of Tunis, directly in front of the Allied approach route. On 17 November, the battalion made contact with the advance guard of the Allied spearhead and a series of battles developed.

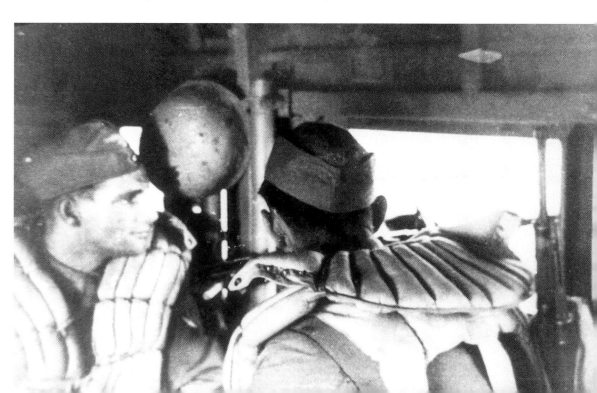

Over the next few days Witzig's men were slowly reinforced, allowing them to pull out of the line and become a reserve unit. Parts of his command then received special training and were given the job of slipping behind enemy lines to carry out reconnaissance and gather intelligence. This intelligence led to the last parachute drop to be carried out by the Fallschirmjäger in North Africa.

The men of the 3rd Company, 11th Parachute Pioneer Battalion, were chosen for the operation and began immediate training. The objectives were airfields and bridges behind Allied lines in the Souk el Arba and Souk el Ahras areas, which were being used by the Allies to transport supplies and reinforcements to the front for an assault on Tunis itself. Though the idea of an airdrop was militarily sound, the actual operation was a disaster.

The Ju 52 aircraft took off from airfields outside Tunis in early December 1942. The night was cold and windy and there was no moon. The aircraft were manned by inexperienced and poorly trained pilots, and consequently the Fallschirmjäger were dropped well away from their targets. This meant a long

Left: *Paratroopers in Tunisia wearing splinter-green camouflage jump smocks and the tropical version of the Fliegermütze (Field Cap). The latter had the Luftwaffe version of the national emblem positioned in the centre of the upper part of the front of the cap, with the black-white-red cockade below it. The tropical overtrousers were very popular with airborne troops, and had a large map pocket on the left leg. There seems little evidence to suggest that a tan-coloured jump smock was ever issued, at least not officially.*

walk once on the ground. In fact the paratroopers never reached their targets, for as soon as they landed they were rounded up by the many British patrols in the area. Within a few days all the pioneers had been captured, many suffering from the effects of the sun. The airborne operation to disrupt the Allied advance on Tunis had been a fiasco (following the fall of Tunisia, the 11th Pioneer Battalion was reformed around a cadre of survivors of the North African campaign, the unit being expanded to become the 21st Parachute Pioneer Regiment, which fought on the Eastern Front and in the West in 1944–45).

Another airborne failure

The failure of the parachute drop did not deter the High Command, who authorised another airborne assault a few days later. This was carried out by gliders on 26 December 1942, when men of the Parachute Company of the Brandenburg Regiment took off to destroy bridges being used as supply routes by the British. This assault also ended in disaster. Some of the gliders were shot down as they passed over enemy lines, while others were downed as they approached their targets. Most of the men were killed in the operation.

At the beginning of 1943 the Axis strategic position in Tunisia was grim. To the west were the British First Army and US II Corps, which were shadowed by Colonel-General Jürgen von Arnim's Fifth Panzer Army. Rommel's Panzer

Below: *These Fallschirmjäger, photographed in Tunisia in early 1943, are members of a reconnaissance unit and are wearing the standard motorcyclists' proofed coat. The Allied superiority in men and material, especially aircraft and artillery, made movement on the ground risky and resulted in heavy casualties among German troops. Though the Fallschirmjäger took the offensive whenever the tactical situation allowed, losses were prohibitive. In early 1943, for example, the 1st Battalion, 5th Parachute Regiment, fought a series of battles in the vicinity of Bou-Arada. Losses were heavy, some companies being reduced to 30 men (standard strength 170 men).*

Army Afrika had made a masterful withdrawal from Egypt and now held the fortified zone at Mareth, with its left flank on the Gulf of Gabes and its right resting on the almost impassable salt marshes of the Chott Djerid. Rommel's attack against the US II Corps at Kasserine (14–22 February) and von Arnim's assault on the First Army's positions in northern Tunisia gained some time, but at the beginning of March Rommel was repulsed before Mareth (he was then to leave Africa due to illness) and the Germans lost the subsequent Battle of Mareth (20–26 March).

Axis forces continued to fight tenaciously, and the paras especially so. There were savage actions at Medjez-el-Bab (where there is a cemetery containing the graves of many fallen Fallschirmjäger) and Tebourba, but it was now impossible to halt the Allied tide. Reinforcements were still being flown into Tunisia, among them the *Barenthin* Parachute Regiment. This unit was an ad hoc formation made up of three battalions and supporting elements drawn from various units. As its commander was Colonel Walter Barenthin, a senior paratrooper engineer, it seems likely that a high proportion of his men were also engineers. Once in Tunisia it was allocated to the *Manteuffel* Division.

The final battle for Tunisia took place in May 1943, when Allied forces pierced the Axis perimeter: II Corps north and south of Lake Bizerta and the

Below: *A Fallschirmjäger motorcycle team asks for directions in Tunis. Motorcycles (this is a BMW 750cc bike and sidecar) were usually attached to a division's reconnaissance company. By the end of March 1943 paratrooper units were trying to slow the Allied advance into Tunisia, which cost them dearly in manpower. Unteroffizier Feigel fought in a typical action at this time: "On 28 March 1943, we deployed in a forest of cork oaks, across which we were ordered to lay mines. As we were getting about the job, the British unleashed a deluge of shells at our positions. The bombing went on for one hour on end. One hour of Hell. Casualties were soon heavy."*

Above: *A hasty conference during the last days of the Tunisian campaign. By the beginning of April 1943 Axis units were in full retreat. Many Fallschirmjäger personnel were taken prisoner, their units often being surrounded by Allied armoured columns. To make matters worse, the paratroopers were suffering grave shortages of ammunition. The final battles in the Tunis sector on 27 April cost the 5th Parachute Regiment over 300 casualties.*

First Army east from Medjez-el-Bab. Von Arnim had committed all his reserves and the Luftwaffe was in the process of withdrawing to Sicily, and was therefore unable to halt the Allied advance. Allied units entered Tunis on 7 May, and French and British forces surrounded the Italian First Army. Axis units began surrendering in droves, and by the end of the campaign (13 May) 275,000 prisoners had been taken. Most of what was left of the *Ramcke* Brigade, *Barenthin* Regiment and 11th Pioneer Battalion entered captivity. Ramcke himself, together with Witzig, Koch and other senior Fallschirmjäger commanders, were airlifted out of Tunisia before the surrender. In the great scheme of things the loss of a few hundred Fallschirmjäger was insignificant, for the Wehrmacht had lost an entire army group in North Africa – Germany's next great military disaster after Stalingrad. On Hitler's southern flank the fighting would now move to Sicily and Italy.

Right: *The Afrika cuff title was instituted on 15 January 1943, and was awarded to personnel who had served for six months in the African theatre. The band was khaki coloured, with the word "AFRIKA" in Roman letters being flanked by two palm trees in silver-grey cotton.*

Above: *General der Flieger Kurt Student inspects Fallschirmjäger in Sicily. He wears the Iron Cross, 1st Class, which he won in World War I, plus the Knight's Cross at his throat.*

ITALY I – BLUNTING THE ALLIED SPEARHEAD

As Italy started to waver as a member of the Axis, then collapsed altogether in the autumn of 1943, Hitler was forced to commit more and more troops and material to protect his southern flank. These resources included the 1st and 4th Parachute Divisions, which fought superbly in defence of Sicily and the Italian mainland.

Left: *A young paratrooper in southern Italy watches Allied aircraft on their way to bomb German positions in late 1943. The fighting on the so-called "soft underbelly of Europe" – the Italian mainland – was to cost a total of 536,000 German and 312,000 Allied casualties.*

Before the campaign in Africa had ended, US President Franklin D. Roosevelt and British Prime Minister Winston Churchill met at Casablanca, Morocco, to devise future military strategy. The next target agreed upon was Sicily. It was not the first choice, and it represented a compromise between US and British strategists. Britain had long-standing political and strategic interests in the Mediterranean, and believed that Sicily's conquest would reopen Allied sealanes to the eastern Mediterranean, provide a base from which to launch further offensives in the region, and might provoke the war-weary Italians into dropping out of the war.

US strategists, led by Army Chief of Staff General George C. Marshall, were keen on a direct thrust against Nazi Germany, specifically a cross-Channel attack. However, the two Allied leaders wished to divert Germany's attention away from the war against the Soviet Union, and were anxious to exploit the momentum of the impending victory in North Africa. In addition, the mass of

Left: *These hungry paratroopers are among the lucky ones that escaped from Tunisia to Sicily following the Axis collapse in North Africa. The first elements of the 1st Parachute Division arrived on the island on 12 July 1943. The 1st, 5th and 6th Companies of the division's 1st Parachute Antitank Battalion arrived a few days later.*

men and equipment that would be available after the end of the war in Africa made an operation in the Mediterranean attractive and logical. After considering actions in Greece, the Balkans, Crete and Sardinia, the Casablanca conference chose Sicily as the next phase of the war against the Axis.

General Dwight D. Eisenhower was selected as the supreme Allied commander for Operation "Husky", the codename for the attack on Sicily, with General Sir Harold Alexander as his deputy and actual commander of Allied land forces during the campaign. Alexander's Fifteenth Army Group would direct Lieutenant-General George S. Patton's US Seventh Army and General Sir Bernard Montgomery's British Eighth Army, the veteran formation of the North African war.

Below: *Operation "Husky", the Allied invasion of Sicily, gets under way. In total, an armada of 2590 vessels were used to launch the attack, and over the succeeding 38 days 500,000 Allied soldiers, sailors and airmen battled for control of the island.*

Below: *A dead Fallschirmjäger on Sicily. Though the 1st Parachute Division and Hermann Göring Division put up spirited resistance, Italian units on the island, many poorly equipped, badly led and having low morale, put up only token resistance at best. By 24 July, Lieutenant-General George S. Patton's US Seventh Army had taken control of the entire western half of the island, capturing 53,000 Italians and 400 vehicles for the loss of 272 men. The worsening situation convinced Berlin that Sicily could not be held, and so General Hans Hube, commander of the newly constituted XIV Panzer Corps, planned a withdrawal to the mainland. The evacuation was complete by 17 August 1943, by which time 29,000 Axis soldiers were dead and a further 140,000 prisoner. By comparison, British dead numbered 2721; US fatalities were 2237.*

The invasion took place along the island's southeastern shore due to the preponderance of favourable beaches, ports and airfields. The key strategic objective of the campaign was the port of Messina in the northeastern corner of the island. The main transit point between Sicily and the Italian mainland, it is surrounded by extremely rugged terrain with narrow beaches. Moreover, it had been heavily fortified and was beyond the range at which Allied Africa-based fighters could provide effective air cover for bombers. It was therefore ruled out as an initial objective.

The plan for the invasion of Sicily

The final Allied plan involved seven divisions: the Eighth Army would land four divisions, an independent brigade and a Commando force from the Pachino Peninsula to just south of the port of Syracuse (a glider landing would assist the amphibious troops in taking Syracuse itself); the Seventh Army would land three divisions in the Gulf of Gela, which would be aided by paratroopers from the US 505th Parachute Infantry Regimental Combat Team and the 3rd Battalion, US 504th Parachute Infantry Regiment. Once ashore, the Eighth Army would drive north to take Augusta, Catania, the airfields at Gerbini and finally Messina. The Seventh Army, in a supporting role, would take airfields

between Licata and Comiso, then protect the west flank of the Eighth Army as it headed towards Messina.

The Axis defenders were under the overall command of General Alfredo Guzzoni's Italian Sixth Army. The 200,000 Italian troops were organised into six coastal divisions, four infantry divisions and a variety of local defence forces. Many were poorly trained and equipped, and their morale was questionable. The 30,000 German troops were grouped in the 15th Panzergrenadier Division and the élite *Hermann Göring* Panzer Division.

The invasion of Sicily

Guzzoni realised his only chance of success was to crush the Allies on the shore before they could consolidate their beachhead. He therefore spread his coastal units in a thin line around the island's perimeter and placed two Italian infantry divisions in the island's western and southeastern corners. He wanted to concentrate the German divisions in the southeast, too, but Field Marshal Albert Kesselring, Hitler's representative in Italy, transferred the bulk of the 15th Panzergrenadier Division to western Sicily before the invasion to cover the eventuality of the Allies landing there. As a result, only the *Hermann Göring* Division was in a position to launch a counterattack during the first few hours of the invasion.

The invasion took place during the night of 9/10 July 1943. Opposition from the dispirited and ill-equipped Italian coastal units was negligible, and by the end of the first day the Eighth Army was on its way to Augusta, having taken Syracuse easily. Resistance in the US sector was not much stronger. The next two days saw resistance stiffen as Guzzoni committed the *Hermann Göring*

Above: *Soldiers of the 2nd Parachute Division fight pro-Badoglio activists in Rome on 9 September 1943, following the Italian capitulation to the Allies the day before. The division had moved to Arles and Nîmes in France in late May 1943 and was subordinated to XI Flieger Corps. In June, it was ordered to Italy, taking up positions guarding the coast between the Tiber estuary and Tarquinia. It was moved to Rome on 9 September as part of the German plan to disarm the Italian garrison and occupy the city. The Italians put up only light resistance, and by the 10th the paras had taken control of the city. At Monte Rotondo, northeast of Rome, the Italian headquarters staff decided to fight. Thus an airdrop by Major Walter Gericke's 2nd Battalion, 6th Parachute Regiment, took place. The Fallschirmjäger operation was a complete success, Gericke's men taking 15 officers and 2000 men prisoner with little effort, an action that earned him the German Cross in Gold.*

Division, but by the 13th the Eighth Army had still advanced as far as Vizzini in the west and Augusta in the east. There, progress slowed due to a combination of difficult terrain and the arrival of the 1st Parachute Division.

The 1st Parachute Division, under the command of Generalmajor Richard Heidrich, was formed from the 7th Flieger Division in May 1943. From the end of May it was stationed in Flers near Avignon, France, coming under the command of XI Flieger Corps, Army Group D. On 11 July the division was ordered to prepare for a move to Sicily, and the next day the first units were air-lifted to Rome. These units were the 1st and 3rd Battalions of the 3rd Parachute Regiment, the 4th Parachute Regiment and the division's machine-gun battalion. Once they arrived in Rome, the 4th Parachute Regiment and the machine-gun battalion were loaded onto gliders and Ju 52 aircraft and dropped around Syracuse and Catania. It would be two days before the 3rd Parachute Regiment was despatched to the island, while the 1st Parachute Regiment was sent to a holding area near Naples to await further orders.

The Fallschirmjäger in Sicily

On Sicily, the German paratroopers set about preparing defensive positions. The machine-gun battalion, backed up by Fallschirmjäger antitank and artillery elements, dug in around Primasole Bridge over the River Simeto in the east of the island. The bridge was an important objective for both sides, highlighted by the fact that several hours after the German paratroopers arrived their adversaries in the British 1st Parachute Brigade (under the command of Brigadier C. W. Lathbury and consisting of the 1st, 2nd, 3rd Battalions and 21st Independent Company – Pathfinders) jumped in on 13 July. A savage battle began, in which the British paras were forced to retreat with some loss.

Fallschirmjäger of the 3rd Parachute Regiment jumped onto Catania air-field on 14 July, which at the time was under fire from Allied aircraft and naval artillery. Meanwhile, the men of the Fallschirmjäger machine-gun battalion, expecting relief, mistook British paras for their own side, and in the confusion the British captured Primasole Bridge. However, the machine-gun battalion

Below: *Fallschirmjäger in southern Italy in late 1943. By this time Allied air strength was making itself felt, a situation amplified by the diminishing strength of the Luftwaffe. On 3 July 1943, for example, the Luftwaffe had a total of 1280 aircraft in the Mediterranean; on 3 September this had fallen to 800. Heinrich Hermsen, 7th Parachute Regiment, was posted near Frascati and witnessed Allied air superiority first-hand: "On 8 September 1943, I witnessed the heavy air attack directed at Generalfeldmarschall Kesselring (who had already left), and later the bombing of Frascati which claimed thousands of lives."*

Above: *The photographs on this and the opposite page show men and vehicles of the 4th Parachute Division, commanded by Generalleutnant Heinrich Trettner, on the move to contain the Allied Anzio bridgehead. Major-General John Lucas' US VI Corps – 50,000 British and US troops – had landed on 22 January 1944.*

Below: *Camouflaging motorcycles as a precaution against being spotted by Allied aircraft. These are BMW vehicles equipped with sidecars for reconnaissance. They are also fitted with towing hooks to pull light antitank or artillery weapons, though such a load severely reduced cross-country performance.*

and the newly arrived 3rd Parachute Regiment mounted a counterattack a few hours later which retook the bridge. The Germans crossed the river to the east, and under attack from three directions the remnants of the 1st Parachute Brigade were forced to withdraw into a small perimeter to the south.

The loss of Primasole Bridge

During the night of 14/15 July the two Fallschirmjäger engineer companies jumped onto Catania airfield. They marched to Primasole Bridge and took up positions on the south side of the bridge. During the morning the British, with the support of tanks of the 4th Armoured Brigade, attacked the bridge again. Again they were flung back by a combination of antitank, machine-gun and mortar fire. The paras came back again, this time reinforced by troops of the Durham Light Infantry, but again they were beaten off by the Germans. The latter had brought up an 88mm gun, but this was subsequently destroyed by intensive Allied artillery fire. The engineers on the south side of the bridge were badly mauled, and by the afternoon Fallschirmjäger casualties had reached a point whereby further defence of the bridge was untenable. Another British attack

finally wrested the bridge from the paras. Two days later the Fallschirmjäger retook Primasole Bridge, before finally losing it on the 18th.

As the remnants of the two engineer companies amalgamated with the 4th Parachute Regiment and retreated, the 3rd Parachute Regiment was cut off and embroiled in fighting around the town of Carlenini. Breaking through the British encirclement, the unit managed to reach the relative safety of German lines. But now time was beginning to run out for the Germans in Sicily. By 24 July the US Seventh Army was in control of the entire western half of the island. Most Italian units were showing little inclination to fight, and even less so when the Italian dictator Benito Mussolini was deposed on 25 July and replaced by Marshal Pietro Badoglio.

Though fighting continued in Sicily, de facto Italian participation ended. Those Axis forces still fighting had decided to make a stand in the island's rugged northeast corner, around the strongpoints along the so-called Etna Line, and Guzzoni still talked of putting up resistance. But his units were disintegrating, and Berlin made the decision to withdraw from the island. From this point General Hans Hube, commander of the newly formed XIV Panzer Corps, led Axis units in Sicily. He began to pull his forces back to evacuate them across the Strait of Messina to the Italian mainland. The paratroopers were detailed to plug any gaps in the Axis line as the evacuation commenced. Elements of the 1st Parachute Regiment were evacuated on 11 August, while all other Fallschirmjäger units had left the island by the 17th, only hours before the first Allied units entered Messina.

With the relatively easy victory on Sicily, Allied planners began to look at an invasion of the Italian mainland. Eisenhower authorised a landing by the

Below: *The eight-wheeled vehicles are Schwere Panzerspähwagen heavy cross-country armoured cars (SdKfz 232). The division was first formed in November 1943 in the Venice area from units of the 2nd Parachute Division, plus ex-members of the Italian Nembo and Folgore Parachute Divisions. In February 1944 it comprised: 10th Parachute Regiment, 11th Parachute Regiment, 12th Parachute Regiment, 4th Parachute Antitank Battalion, 4th Parachute Artillery Regiment, 4th Parachute Antiaircraft Battalion, 4th Parachute Engineer Battalion, 4th Parachute Signals Battalion, and 4th Parachute Medical Battalion.*

Eighth Army, codenamed "Baytown", on 16 August. The assault would take place across the Strait of Messina between 1 and 4 September to tie down enemy units that might interfere with US landings farther north. The latter, Operation "Avalanche", would take place on 9 September when the US Fifth Army went ashore in the Salerno area. Both armies were grouped under the Allied Fifteenth Army Group, commanded by General Sir Harold Alexander.

German plans for the defence of Italy

In view of the wavering Italian war effort, Hitler had given Kesselring, Commander-in-Chief South, the responsibility of defending southern Italy. Kesselring at the time was thinking of fighting a delaying action until he could establish a permanent defensive line in the Apennine mountains north of Rome. However, in the event of Italy deserting the Axis, Hitler had given Field Marshal Erwin Rommel, commander of Army Group B, responsible for the defence of northern Italy, the task of occupying all important mountain passes, roads and railways and disarming the Italians. Kesselring, meanwhile, would disarm the Italians in the south and continue withdrawing north.

In mid-August 102,000 Axis troops withdrew from Sicily to the mainland, and on 8 August the German Tenth Army was established under the command of General Heinrich von Vietinghoff. Its 45,000 men had the task of defending the toe of Italy in conjunction with the Italian Seventh Army. Vietinghoff had three German divisions: the *Hermann Göring* Division, 15th Panzergrenadier Division and 16th Panzer Division.

Above: *B25Bs of the US Twelfth Army Air Force en route to bomb German positions at Anzio. The Fourteenth Army, commanded by General Hans Georg Mackensen, reacted quickly to contain and then attack the bridgehead. The 4th Parachute Division soon established itself as one of the toughest units in the German order of battle, as recorded in the army's battle reports: 7 February: "4th Parachute Division ... reached their designated objectives in all sectors"; 16 February: "The 16th Infantry Division and the 4th Parachute Division seized the ridge south of Cle Buon Riposo."*

Right: *Fallschirmjäger of the 4th Parachute Division mounted on an SdKfz 251 semi-tracked medium armoured personnel carrier near Anzio. They are wearing a mixture of paratrooper and army helmets and flight caps. By the end of February 1944, the division was suffering heavy losses due to continuous combat. Its commander, Trettner, led by example and was mentioned several times in Wehrmacht despatches for his bravery. Over 10,000 SdKfz 251s were built during the war. The gun shield at the front of the vehicle mounted an MG 34 or 42 machine gun.*

Below: *German paratroopers on patrol at Anzio. Between March and April the battle for the bridgehead turned into a siege, with all positions of the narrow bridgehead being under continuous observation and fire, while the Luftwaffe strafed the harbour area, disrupting supply and reinforcement efforts. Nevertheless, Allied attacks became more numerous. A Fourteenth Army report of 9 March is typical: "Enemy attacks against the 10th Parachute Regiment's right flank by about two companies, launched after two hours of artillery preparation, were repelled in hard fighting."*

The British Eighth Army crossed the Strait of Messina on 3 September, and on the same day the Italian Badoglio government signed a secret armistice agreement. The formal announcement of the Italian surrender was made on 8 September, prompting German units to move quickly to disarm their former allies (they had moved into jumping-off positions earlier).

In late July, the newly raised 2nd Parachute Division had been moved from its base in southern France to a coastal area between the Tiber estuary and Tarquinia. This was in anticipation of any unrest in Rome. Under the command of Generalmajor Bernhard Ramcke, it was composed of the 2nd Parachute Regiment, an artillery battalion from the remnants of Ramcke's brigade that served in North Africa, and the 4th Battalion of the Luftlande-Sturmregiment (Airlanding Assault Regiment). In addition, the Fallschirmjäger Lehr Battalion (Parachute Training Battalion) was used as a cadre to form the new 6th and 7th Parachute Regiments. On 9 September the 2nd Parachute Division was ordered into the city to undertake Operation "Student": restore order, disarm the Italian troops of the Rome garrison and occupy the city. This had been achieved by the 10th.

Resistance was heavier at Monte Rotondo, northeast of Rome, which was the headquarters of the Italian Army and its general staff and who refused to surrender to the Germans. A drop by Major Walter Gericke's 2nd Battalion, 6th

Parachute Regiment, onto the Italian headquarters brought all resistance to an end. Casualties were light.

The US Fifth Army went ashore at Salerno on 9 September, and despite German pressure the beachhead was firmly established by the end of the month. By that time the Allies had brought 190,000 troops ashore and were pushing north. In response, Kesselring had established a series of defensive lines across the Italian peninsula. The first was the Barbara Line, a hastily built number of fortifications along the River Volturno, 40km (25 miles) north of Naples. The second was through Migano, extending east from the coast to Monte Camino, Monte Maggiore and Monte Sammucro. It was called the Bernhard or Reinhard Line. The third line, 19.2km (12 miles) north of the Bernhard Line and anchored on Monte Cassino and the Garigliano and Rapido Rivers, was called the Gustav Line. Composed of interlocking bunkers and fortifications, it was the strongest of the three lines.

The formation of I Parachute Corps

On 21 November 1943, Kesselring was made commander of Army Group C responsible for the whole of Italy (Rommel was transferred to France). At the same time, two German armies were formed under Army Group C: Tenth Army under General von Vietinghoff, and Fourteenth Army under General von Mackensen. The parachute units in Italy also underwent a reorganisation at this time. I Parachute Corps was formed in January 1944. Under the control of General Alfred Schlemm, it would control the 1st and 4th Parachute Divisions throughout the war in Italy. The 4th Parachute Division began forming in November 1943. It was created around the 1st Battalion, 2nd Parachute Regiment; 2nd Battalion, 6th Parachute Regiment; and the 1st Battalion, Luftlande-Sturmregiment. In addition, Italian troops from the Nembo and Folgore Parachute Divisions joined it. The division was complete by January 1944.

Above: *On the road to Anzio. Eventually the number of Allied troops in the bridgehead numbered 110,000, while the Germans massed 70,000 men to contain them. The Allies also deployed élite units at Anzio, which the Fallschirmjäger encountered. Oberleutnant Opel, Parachute Training Regiment, states: "To check a force of Rangers who had thrust into the positions held by a neighbouring company, I launched at one of their flanks, thus cutting off large numbers of Americans from their unit. About 4–500 Americans fell into our hands."*

Meanwhile, the month-long struggle from Salerno to the Bernhard Line had all but exhausted the Fifth and Eighth Armies by mid-November 1943. To break the stalemate, it was proposed to land the US VI Corps behind enemy lines at Anzio. The Allied offensive in Italy resumed on 20 November, but bad weather and German resistance inhibited progress. Nevertheless, in mid-January the Allied armies were through the first two German defence lines and were facing the Gustav Line. To facilitate the amphibious landings, the Fifth Army would attack towards the Rapido and Garigliano Rivers. Operation "Shingle", the landings at Anzio, commenced on 22 January 1944 unopposed. The US Fifth Army's offensive, however, encountered stiff resistance, especially around Cassino and the Benedictine monastery on Monte Cassino above the town (see Chapter 8).

At Anzio, Major-General John Lucas dug in to secure the bridgehead before launching an offensive. This meant that by 30 January the Germans were able to mass 70,000 troops around Anzio and effectively stall the attack on Rome (had the Allies pressed forward immediately from the beachhead, the Germans might have been hard-pressed to stop them). As it was, von Mackensen was able to deploy his Fourteenth Army to contain the beachhead. In addition, Kesselring ordered that all combat troops that could be spared from the Tenth

Right: *A wounded survivor of the 4th Parachute Division trudges back from a field dressing station. By the end of May 1944 the Fourteenth Army, having failed to reduce the bridgehead, was facing defeat at Anzio. By 25 May the US Fifth Army had established contact with units in the bridgehead, and the Germans were retreating north. As ever, the Fallschirmjäger were covering the withdrawal. 29 May: "The 4th Parachute Division and 65th Infantry Division repelled several attacks, but the enemy succeeded in penetrating the line." (Fourteenth Army battle report)*

Army should be transferred to the Anzio Front. These included the Headquarters of I Parachute Corps, the 3rd Battalion of the 1st Parachute Regiment, 1st Parachute Division, and the Machine Gun Battalion of the 1st Parachute Division.

Hard-fought actions at Anzio

Around Anzio three divisional sectors were initially established – Western Sector, Centre Sector and Eastern Sector – all under the command of I Parachute Corps. The 4th Parachute Division was in command of the Western Sector, and was deployed south of the River Tiber near Terracina. At this time the staff of the division was still being activated.

By the end of the month I Parachute Corps had devised an attack, but the Germans were already feeling the effects of Allied air superiority, as a Fourteenth Army report dated 29 January makes clear: "The main mission of the Fourteenth Army is to annihilate the beachhead, which the enemy is rein-forcing. The attack must be made as soon as possible; the date depends on the arrival of the necessary forces, which is being delayed, as the railroad system in Italy has been crippled by enemy air raids." On 30 January, US Rangers were forced back from Cisterna, leaving supporting British troops in an exposed position. Further German attacks between 3–4 February inflicted heavy losses on the Allies, and by the 13th the invaders were virtually back on their last defence lines along the Albano–Anzio road.

A period of relative inactivity then descended as Mackensen prepared his last great attack. Morale among the Allied troops was very low, and it seemed possible to the Germans that the beachhead could be eliminated. The main attack began at dawn on 16 February. The 4th Parachute Division, along with

Below: *The breaching of the Gustav Line precipitated a full-scale retreat by the German Tenth and Fourteenth Armies in Italy. On 2 June Kesselring was forced to order all German units to break off contact with the enemy and pull back north. He declared Rome an open city the next day, ignoring Hitler's orders to use explosives to blow up large areas of the metropolis. These Fallschirmjäger were among the last to leave. During the night of 4 June, units of the US 1st Special Service Force, 1st Armored Division and the 3rd, 34th, 36th, 85th and 88th Infantry Divisions entered Rome. The first Axis capital had fallen.*

Right: *Beaten certainly but not bowed, Fallschirmjäger head north from Rome in June 1944. By 21 June they had been pushed 176km (110 miles) up the peninsula. Then Allied units halted in late July for rest and refitting, giving the Germans time to complete their Gothic Line defences.*

the 65th Infantry Division, seized the ridge south of Cle Buon Riposo. Allied artillery and air attacks were heavy, but the Germans forged on, seemingly oblivious to casualties. However, massive Allied air and artillery strikes halted the attack on 19 February. Further fighting continued, but by the end of the month Mackensen had halted his attacks at Anzio. He complained to Kesselring of the "insufficient training of troops, and your replacements, who are not qualified to meet the Allied troops in battle. Due to this, the Army will be unable to wipe out the beachhead with the troops at hand".

Battles of attrition

The beachhead had been saved but the fighting continued. A German operational report dated 2–4 March, for example, recorded: "Due to strong enemy counterattacks, one company of the 4th Parachute Division, which had occupied the eastern part of the Ciocca gorge, was wiped out by the enemy." Four days later, the 10th Parachute Regiment's right flank was hit by two enemy companies, and the attack was only beaten off after heavy fighting. By the beginning of April, the 4th Parachute Division had been weakened so much by the fighting that a Fourteenth Army summary concerning the fighting qualities of its units placed it in Combat Quality Classification II.

Farther south, the Allies had failed three times to break the Gustav Line: in January against the Rapido River; in February with the attempt to outflank Cassino; and in March with the attempt to drive between the monastery on Monte Cassino and the town below. However, the Fifteenth Army Group embarked upon a massive build-up and intensive aerial campaign to prepare the ground for a fresh offensive. Codenamed Operation "Diadem", it opened on 11 May 1944 with a massive barrage by 1600 artillery pieces along the entire front, followed by an assault by 25 Allied divisions. Progress in the Eighth Army's sector was slow, but the Americans made better headway. On 25 May Allied troops from Anzio linked up with patrols of the US Fifth Army north of Terracina — four months after the original landing. The 4th Parachute Division fought a series of savage rearguard actions as Mackensen retreated north, but the momentum was with the Allies and there was nothing the Germans could do to stop Rome falling on 4 June. The first Axis capital had fallen. But there was still a lot of fighting left to do in Italy.

Above: *Keeping watch in the Cassino sector. Note the helmet cover of this Fallschirmjäger, which is manufactured from Italian Army camouflage material, plus his Iron Cross ribbon.*

BLOOD BATH AT CASSINO

At the beginning of 1944, the US Fifth Army and British Eighth Army were ready to launch their first major effort against the Gustav Line, link up with a projected amphibious landing at Anzio and then sweep on to Rome. Five months of bitter fighting ensued, as the Fallschirmjäger refused to budge from a place that would enter military legend – Monte Cassino.

Left: *Clearly showing the strains of combat, these men of the 1st Parachute Division take an opportunity to grab a few moments of rest from the perils of combat at Monte Cassino. Much of the fighting in Cassino and around Monte Cassino itself was at close quarters and often hand-to-hand.*

Of all the Fallschirmjäger actions in World War II, it was the battles to hold the monastery of Monte Cassino and the town of Cassino below that have entered military folklore. The men of the 1st Parachute Division earned the title "The Green Devils of Cassino" for their performance during a battle described by Hitler as being "a battle of the First World War fought with weapons of the second".

At the beginning of 1944 the Allies accelerated plans for an amphibious landing behind German lines at Anzio, to be undertaken by the US Fifth Army's VI Corps (see Chapter 7). In the same month the newly formed French Expeditionary Corps under General Alphonse Juin had arrived and took up position on the Fifth Army's eastern flank, with the US II Corps in the centre and the British X Corps in support. The Fifth Army was ordered to break through enemy lines to link up with the beachhead, but to do so it had to breach the Gustav Line. The latter lay along two rivers – the Garigliano and the Rapido

— and the Fifth Army would draw enemy forces away from Anzio by attacking towards the two rivers, crossing them, taking the high ground on both sides of the Liri Valley, and then driving north to link up with the beachhead. The British Eighth Army, commanded by Lieutenant-General Sir Oliver Leese, would support these operations by crossing the River Sangro and taking Pescara, further tying down the enemy.

First assault on Monte Cassino

The Liri Valley is a long, flat plain through which flowed Highway 6, the main north-south road to Rome. Unfortunately for the Allies, the Germans had fortified every key point in the valley and they held the heights which guarded the mouth of the valley: Monte Cassino and Monte Majo. The Allied assault began on 17 January. II Corps' 36th Infantry Division spearheaded the crossing of the Rapido near Sant'Angelo, but the failure of X Corps and the French Expeditionary Corps to dislodge the Germans from the heights on both sides of the Liri Valley meant the attack failed with heavy casualties. All attempts to cross the Rapido had ended by 22 January, but the necessity of relieving the Anzio beachhead forced Clark to renew his attacks.

The new assault took place over the high ground northeast of the town of Cassino. The British X Corps resumed its attack from the Garigliano bridgehead, while the US 34th Infantry Division, with the help of the French Expeditionary Corps and a regiment of the 36th Infantry Division, endeavoured to outflank Cassino and storm the Benedictine monastery on Monte Cassino above the town. The result was that US and French units gained a precarious foothold on the northeastern slopes of Monte Cassino itself, while the 34th Infantry Division had crossed the Rapido by 26 January.

In early February 1944, the 34th Infantry Division renewed its attacks on Cassino to prepare for another attempt at the Liri Valley by the recently created New Zealand Corps under Lieutenant-General Sir Bernard Freyberg. However, after days of savage fighting the Germans still held the town, and the New Zealand Corps relieved the Americans.

Thus far the Allies had spared the monastery from air, artillery and ground attacks, even though it was a crucial strategic point. However, sightings of German troops within its walls, plus enemy emplacements and strongpoints

Above: *The monastery of Monte Cassino being bombed by Allied aircraft on 15 February 1944. One result of the bombing and shelling of the hill and town of Cassino was to create cover for the German paratroopers and more problems for the attackers. It would take a lot to dislodge the paratroopers, as Major Rudolf Böhmler, the commander of the 1st Battalion, 3rd Parachute Regiment, 1st Parachute Division, later stated: "One must appreciate that the fighting at Cassino was mountain warfare; and in mountain warfare the inevitable rule is that whoever is master of the hill is master of the valley." At Cassino the 1st Parachute Division comprised: Divisional Headquarters (General Heidrich); 1st Parachute Regiment (Oberst Schultz), made up of the 1st Battalion (Major von der Schulenburg); 2nd Battalion (Major Groschke); and 3rd Battalion (Major Becker). The 3rd Parachute Regiment, commanded by Oberst Heilmann, comprised: 1st Battalion (Major Böhmler); 2nd Battalion (Major Foltin); and 3rd Battalion (Major Kratzert). The 4th Parachute Regiment, commanded by Oberst Walther, comprised: 1st Battalion (Hauptmann Beyer); 2nd Battalion (Hauptmann Hubner); and 3rd Battalion (Hauptmann Maier). Other divisional elements comprised: 1st Parachute Artillery Regiment (Major Schramm); 1st Pioneer Battalion (Hauptmann Fromming); 1st Parachute Antitank Battalion (Major Bruckner); 1st Parachute Machine Gun Battalion (Major Schmidt) and the Parachute Medical Section (Oberst Dr. Eiben).*

Right: *The Allied bombing of the monastery did not kill the German defenders. The ruins were assaulted between 16–18 February by units of the Indian 7th Brigade. They were summarily repulsed by a combination of artillery and Fallschirmjäger small-arms fire.*

nearby, prompted Freyberg to request its reduction by air and artillery attack. This took place on 15 February, when 230 bombers and II Corps' artillery pounded the historic site. However, though much of the monastery and its outer walls were destroyed, the bombing did not destroy the subterranean chambers where the defenders were sheltering. Thus when the 4th Indian Division attacked on the night of 15 February it was repulsed with heavy loss. The next three days witnessed further Indian assaults, all to no avail and with considerable casualties. Though the 2nd New Zealand Division, supported by the artillery of the 34th and 36th Infantry Divisions, had made some headway into Cassino itself, the terrible losses halted further operations.

The ensuing lull in the fighting gave the Germans an opportunity to reorganise the defences. On 20 February, Generalmajor Richard Heidrich's 1st Parachute Division moved into Cassino and the monastery. The town itself was occupied by

Right: *Generalmajor Richard Heidrich (standing) with Field Marshal Albert Kesselring in the Italian theatre, mid-1944. Heidrich assumed command of the Cassino sector on 20 February 1944, with Cassino and Monte Cassino being entrusted to Oberst Heilmann's 3rd Parachute Regiment (Heilmann would assume command of the 5th Parachute Division on 17 November 1944). The Third Battle of Cassino commenced on 15 March, when a total of 775 Allied aircraft bombed Cassino and its immediate vicinity, hitting German artillery, supply centres and bridges. As soon as the aircraft had finished, Allied artillery opened up. The bombardment of the town lasted till 15:30 hours, but for the ruins of the monastery it went on into the early hours of 16 March. One Fallschirmjäger commander, Hauptmann Foltin, moved his 6th Company into a nearby cave as soon as the shelling started. His initiative saved the company from destruction, and he would later win the Knight's Cross for knocking out 10 enemy tanks and holding an exposed position between 15–20 March.*

the 3rd Parachute Regiment under Oberst Ludwig Heilmann. The division itself was not at full strength, having suffered in the fighting round Ortona. The average fighting strength of its battalions, for example, was around 200 men.

Citadel of stone

Monte Cassino stands 518.2m (1700ft) above sea level, and it dominates the surrounding countryside and what was Route 6, which snakes around Monastery Hill. It looks down on the town of Cassino, but is not the only high point in the area. In fact it is surrounded by other peaks and hills, all of which were to be the scene of heavy fighting. Directly behind the town stood Castle Hill, on the top of which was a dilapidated fort known to the Allies as Point 193, or Rocca Janula. Hangman's Hill, or Point 435, was on the slopes of Monte Cassino itself, while 1km (.625 miles) to the northwest was Point 593, or Calvary Hill. To the north of Calvary stood Snakeshead Hill, or Point 445.

For the next offensive the Allies assembled a massive arsenal. The commander-in-chief of Allied air forces in the Mediterranean, General Eaker, had been instructed to use every available bomber in theatre in the attack, while the quartermaster of the US Fifth Army had gathered 600,000 artillery shells for ground support purposes. Freyberg intended to use both the 4th Indian Division and the 2nd New Zealand Division in one small area for the attack.

Above: *In the ruins of Cassino. Life for the defenders was hazardous to say the least. Rubble littered the area and often buried paratroopers alive. One survivor of the 1st Parachute Division stationed in the monastery describes a typical day during the fighting: "the sun lost its brightness and an uncanny twilight descended. It was like the end of the world. Comrades were wounded, buried alive, dug out again and buried for a second time. Whole platoons and squads were obliterated by direct hits. Scattered survivors half crazy from the explosions reeled about in a daze until they were hit by an explosion or disappeared. Others rushed headlong into the enemy in order to escape from this hell."*

Left: *"We had numerous individual weapons such as rifles, submachine guns, hand grenades and antitank guns. Unfortunately, all our heavy equipment was destroyed during the air and artillery bombings which the Allies had unleashed at Cassino and its surroundings." (Oberjäger Kush, 1st Parachute Antitank Battalion)*

The New Zealanders were to take Cassino and Point 193. The Indians were tasked with storming the steep sides of Monte Cassino and capturing the monastery. The British 78th Division was to cross the Rapido each side of Sant'Angelo in Theodice and push ahead into the Liri Valley.

The Third Battle of Cassino

The aerial bombardment began at 08:30 hours on 15 March and ceased at 12:30 hours. It was followed by a mass artillery barrage involving 746 guns, which fired over 200,000 shells on the town and hill. The 2nd Battalion of the 3rd Parachute Regiment, commanded by Major Foltin, was stationed in the town and took the brunt of the attack. Out of 300 men around 160 were killed, wounded or buried under the debris. The 2nd New Zealand Division, supported by armour, then began its assault, and immediately ran into intense and heavy fire. This was totally unexpected, as the Allies had believed that any defenders still alive after the air and artillery attack would be so shattered psychologically that they would be incapable of further resistance.

By the evening the New Zealanders had captured Point 193 but had failed to dislodge the Fallschirmjäger from the town, especially those in the Hotel Excelsior and around the railway station. In addition, the bombardment had churned up the ground so much that Allied tanks were unable to support the infantry. In addition, Heidrich directed fire from the division's artillery regiment and the 71st Mortar Regiment around Cassino. The latter, plus a detachment of 88mm antiaircraft guns near Aquino, were particularly useful in blunting the New Zealand attack.

The 4th Indian Division advanced over Point 193 during the evening of 15 March and up to Point 165. This created a gap in the defences of Monte Cassino, at the time in the hands of the 1st Battalion, 3rd Parachute Regiment, as the 2nd Company of the battalion had been wiped out on Point 193. Indian troops tried, and failed, to take Point 236, while a detachment of Gurkhas captured Point 435, within 400m (1312ft) of the monastery itself. In Cassino the

Below: *A motorcycle team in the ruins of Cassino. On 19 March, the Fallschirmjäger destroyed 17 New Zealand tanks on the slopes of Monte Cassino in desperate, close-quarter combat. Their dogged resistance prompted Prime Minister Winston Churchill to inquire of General Alexander on 20 March why no progress had been made at Cassino. The general replied that the bombardment had seriously reduced the ability of tanks to operate in the town. He also paid tribute to the powers of endurance and resistance of the German paratroopers, who had withstood a massive artillery bombardment and air assault by the entire Allied air strength in the Italian theatre.*

railway station was captured by Allied troops on 17 March, which meant the town was all but encircled. The Fallschirmjäger mounted a counterattack from the monastery on the night of 18/19 March when the 1st Battalion of the 4th Parachute Regiment attacked Point 193. After heavy fighting, however, the paras were forced to retire.

The savage resistance prompted Alexander to hold a conference on 21 March to consider a halt in the offensive. Freyberg opposed this, but fresh New Zealand attacks the next day brought no success and so Alexander halted the battle the same day. The temporary cessation of hostilities allowed both sides to reorganise. The Allies launched Operation "Strangle" in the third week in March: an air campaign designed to disrupt German supply routes by bombing bridges, roads and railways. Meanwhile, the German Tenth Army was regrouped. The overall command from the Tyrrhenian coast up to the River Liri was entrusted to XIV Panzer Corps, commanded by General von Senger-

Left: *A major reason for the success of the paratroopers at Cassino was the courage and initiative of junior commanders. Oberleutnant Siegfried Jamrowski, 6th Company, 3rd Parachute Regiment, was one such leader. In mid-March his regiment was defending the town of Cassino. After heavy shelling it took 12 hours to dig Jamrowski out of the rubble. Taking command of his company and the 8th Company, he slowed the enemy's advance and formed a new defence line, thereby securing the flanks of those Fallschirmjäger units deployed in the central and southwestern areas of the town. His quick thinking prevented the fall of the town and earned him a Knight's Cross.*

Above: *The Fourth Battle of Cassino opened on 11 May 1944. The Polish 15th Carpathian Brigade, part of the Polish 3rd Division, captured the important Mount Calvary, but lost it after four desperate assaults by German paratroopers. Major Kurt Veth, 3rd Parachute Regiment, recording the nature of the fighting in his diary: "Great number of dead on the slope: stench, no water, no sleep, amputations being carried out at battle headquarters."*

Etterlin, while the divisions between the Liri and Alfedena were placed under General Feuerstein's LI Mountain Corps. The Cassino area was still defended by the 1st Parachute Division, but the 4th Parachute Regiment now occupied the town and monastery hill itself. The 3rd Parachute Regiment was deployed to the northwest. The 1st Parachute Regiment, with two panzergrenadier battalions attached, was held in the rear as a divisional reserve.

The Allied Fifteenth Army Group also regrouped its units. The French Expeditionary Corps was moved to the upper reaches of the Garigliano, where it had taken over the British X Corps' bridgehead. General Anders' Polish II Corps moved into the hills north of Cassino, while the US II Corps (the 85th and 88th Divisions) stood ready on the lower Garigliano. The New Zealand Corps was relieved by the British XIII Corps with the Canadian I Corps behind

Right: *A German tank at Cassino. The men of XIV Panzer Corps were expert in using buildings as shelters in which their tanks could hide. Allied armour could also be devastating. During the Fourth Battle of Cassino, for example, the British 2nd Armoured Brigade, supporting the assault of the 15th Carpathian Brigade, wiped out the paratroopers of the 3rd Company, 3rd Parachute Regiment.*

it. The British X Corps was shifted to the upper Rapido, and so a major part of the British Eighth Army was assembled in the Cassino area.

Preceded by the usual massive aerial and artillery bombardment, the Fifth and Eighth Armies began their attacks on 11 May 1944 – the Fourth Battle of Cassino had begun. Allied gains to the south of the Cassino area were good, especially in the French sector. However, Anders' corps was having a hard time of it. His 5th Division had attacked on the night of 11/12 May towards Sant'Angelo but was repulsed with loss. His 3rd Division had taken Point 593, but throughout 12 May the German paratroopers attacked the Poles and threw them off the hill. The Poles attacked again on 13 and 14 May, but a combination of Fallschirmjäger doggedness and German artillery defeated them. In addition, the German gunners had observation posts on the 914m (3000ft) peak of Monte Cifalco, which commanded a view of the entire offensive area of II

Above: Fallschirmjäger in the final days at Cassino. "On 17 May, with General Guillaume's Moroccans already 25 miles [40km] through the front, General Anders renewed his attacks on the 1st Parachute Division. In a battle which raged hither and thither for 10 hours, possession of Mount Calvary was contested with particular violence. Once more the brave Poles suffered extremely high losses, and still failed to achieve their aim. Equally unsuccessful were all the attempts by the British 4th Division to seize the town of Cassino in the face of resistance put up by the German 4th Parachute Regiment." (Rudolf Böhmler)

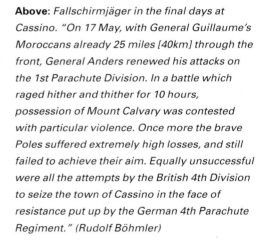

Left: The rocky, coverless terrain around Monte Cassino aided the defenders and ensured attackers suffered heavy casualties. In addition, the Germans were in control of the heights of Monte Cifalco to the north, which gave a view of the entire offensive area of the Polish II Corps.

Above: *A lone British soldier escorts two German prisoners into captivity after the fall of Cassino and the monastery in May 1944. With the breakthrough of the French Expeditionary Corps and the US II Corps farther south, the German Tenth Army was threatened with encirclement from this direction. Thus Field Marshal Kesselring gave orders on 17 May for the entire Cassino front to be evacuated. During the following night the 1st Parachute Division started to pull back west over the mountains. During the morning of 18 May the Poles stormed the ruins of the monastery. The losses on both sides in the Cassino sector amounted to a massive 200,000 killed and wounded. General Harold Alexander had the following to say of the Fallschirmjäger defenders of Cassino: "There are no other troops in the world who would defend their positions with the same obduracy and courage. These are bold and highly trained men, hardened through numerous engagements and campaigns."*

Polish Corps. Developments on the right flank of the 1st Parachute Division, though, were causing the Germans concern.

On 17 May units of the British XIII Corps took Piumarola and reached the Via Casilina, effectively severing the rear communications of the parachute division. Worse were the activities of the French, who had taken Monte Petrella by 16 May and were just south of Pico on 19 May. The Germans were reeling as the US II Corps took Formia (17 May) and Monte Grande (19 May). Monte Cassino was now the last pillar in the German defence line.

General Anders resumed his attack on 17 May, heralding the beginning of a 10-hour battle for possession of Mount Calvary. All Polish attacks were defeated by the paratroopers, who likewise destroyed all attempts by the British 4th Division to take the town below. The "Green Devils of Cassino" were putting up an heroic fight. The irony was that Monte Cassino had long lost its tactical significance. Due to deep penetrations by the French Expeditionary Corps and US II Corps, the Tenth Army was threatened by encirclement from the south (it had lost 40 percent of its combat strength in three days). On 17 May Kesselring issued orders that the entire Cassino front be evacuated, and during the following night the 1st Parachute Division began its retreat west over the mountains. When troops of the Polish 12th Podolski Regiment stormed the ruins of the monastery early in the morning of 18 May, all they found was a group of seriously wounded paras who could not be evacuated.

Losses had been heavy: the Germans had lost 25,000 men in the defence of the Cassino sector, while the Poles had lost 1000 killed in the attacks on Monte Cassino alone. The 1st Parachute Division, battered but defiant, was able to make a successful withdrawal to fight farther north as Germans forces retreated. It left behind a legend.

Above: *A Fallschirmjäger 50mm Pak 38 in action against US tanks in Italy. Note the army helmet on the ground and the variety of jump smocks being worn by the gun crew.*

ITALY II: THE FIGHTING WITHDRAWAL

After their heroics at Cassino and Anzio, the Fallschirmjäger divisions in Italy retreated north to take up positions alongside their German Army companions on the Gothic Line. By the second half of 1944 the Allies enjoyed heavy superiority in manpower and material in Italy, but there was still a lot of hard fighting to do, especially against the veteran paratroopers.

Left: *A paratrooper machine-gun team in action in the hills of northern Italy in 1944. The press-stud fasteners on the lower edge of the jump smock can clearly be seen. The gloved hand on the right presumably belongs to an officer or NCO who is directing the firing.*

By the end of the first week of August 1944, the British Eighth Army stood on the Ponte Vecchio, bridging the Arno River in recently liberated Florence, Italy. In conjunction with the US Fifth Army it had just completed a campaign that had kept Axis forces in Italy in full retreat, and Allied leaders were optimistic that they were on the verge of pushing the Germans out of the northern Apennines, sweeping through the Po Valley beyond, and advancing into the Alps, the Balkans and perhaps Austria.

The Allies had liberated Rome in June 1944, and in a two-month summer campaign had pushed the enemy 240km (150 miles) north to the River Arno. Allied forces then ran into the Gothic Line, a series of fortified passes and mountain tops 24–48km (15–30 miles) in depth north of the Arno, stretching east from the Ligurian Sea through Pisa, Florence and beyond. Farther east, along the Adriatic coast where the northern Apennines slope down onto a broad coastal plain, Gothic Line defences were anchored on the many rivers, streams and other waterways flowing from the mountains to the sea. The city of Bologna was the key to the line, being a major rail and road communications hub just to the north of the defensive belt.

With the loss of several veteran divisions to the northwestern theatre after the Allied invasion of France on 6 June 1944, once the British and Americans had reached the Gothic Line they might have remained there for the rest of the war. However, this would allow Axis commanders to hold their positions with a minimal force, thus freeing units for duty elsewhere. In addition, British Prime Minister Winston Churchill was becoming increasingly alarmed at the speed of Soviet advances on the Eastern Front, which he felt threatened Western interests in Eastern Europe and British interests in the Mediterranean. He therefore wanted to press on into the Po Valley, push east into the Balkans and north through the Ljubljana Gap, reaching the Danube Valley, Austria and Hungary before the Red Army (at this time the Americans did not share Churchill's concerns about Soviet intentions or his enthusiasm for campaigns in Eastern

Left: *An 80mm mortar in action on the Gothic Line. The GrW 34 mortar was used by German troops on all fronts, and proved to be very accurate. In the hands of a highly trained team it could fire up to 25 rounds a minute. Weighing 62kg (136.4lb), it was usually served by a crew of three. There were a number of variants, including the GrW 42 Stummelwerfer (see Chapter 2). The shorter barrel meant that the range was reduced from 2400m (7990ft) down to 1100m (3660ft). It was ready for service in 1943, though by this time the paratrooper divisions were fighting as ground troops. As a result, only 1591 were produced, all in 1943.*

Above: *The photographs on this page show members of the 4th Parachute Division with Italian paratroopers in 1944. Sizeable numbers of Italians from the Folgore and Nembo Parachute Divisions joined the division after the Italian armistice with the Allies. These men later fought well beside their German comrades, proving that Italian troops could perform in combat just as well as other soldiers when given the right equipment and leadership.*

Europe). However, the Allies did plan to continue offensive operations in the northern Apennines in the hope of breaking through the Gothic Line.

In August 1944, Field Marshal Sir Harold Alexander commanded the Fifteenth Army Group. This comprised Lieutenant-General Mark Clark's US Fifth Army, made up of IV Corps and II Corps, which held the western portion of the Allied line from the Ligurian Sea at the mouth of the Arno River to a point just west of Florence. To the east was Lieutenant-General Sir Oliver Leese's larger Eighth Army, made up of the Polish II Corps, Canadian I Corps, and British V, X and XIII Corps. It held a line from the Florence area to just south of Fano on the Adriatic coast.

Axis forces in Italy, grouped under Army Group C, were commanded by Field Marshal Albert Kesselring. Opposing Clark's US Fifth Army was

Right: *Italian and German members of the 4th Parachute Division. This photograph shows the mixture of clothing that had become typical in Fallschirmjäger units towards the end of the war in Italy (from left to right): infantry helmet with old grey-green jump smock, and Italian paratroop helmet with German splinter-pattern jump smock.*

Lieutenant-General Joachim Lemelsen's Fourteenth Army, which contained 10 divisions belonging to I Parachute and XIV Panzer Corps. Farther east, opposite the British Eighth Army, was the Tenth Army under General Heinrich von Vietinghoff. It consisted of 12 divisions belonging to LXXVI Panzer and LI Mountain Corps. Other Axis forces in northern Italy comprised the Ligurian Army and the Adriatic Command, which undertook numerous anti-partisan and reserve missions.

General Leese advocated the Eighth Army attacking up the Adriatic coast to Rimini to draw Axis units away from the Fifth Army's front. Clark could then attack the Gothic Line in a secondary assault from Florence directly north towards Bologna, and both armies could then converge on and capture Bologna itself and move to encircle and destroy Axis forces in the Po Valley. The operation was codenamed "Olive".

The operation began on 25 August 1944 with the British V Corps and Canadian I Corps attacking along the Adriatic. Supported by the British Desert

Below: *In the turret of a tank. In the Italian campaign the Germans buried some tanks in the ground up to their turrets, creating antitank emplacements. Gefreiter Herbert Fries, for example, of the 1st Parachute Antitank Battalion, manning the gun of one such vehicle, helped cover the retreat of the 1st Parachute Division from the Cassino sector. Stationed west of Piedimonte, between 21–23 May 1944 Fries knocked out 20 Sherman tanks, an exploit which won him the Knight's Cross.*

Above: *A paratrooper dashes for cover during the German retreat in Italy in the second half of 1944. During this period the commander of the 1st Parachute Division, Generalmajor Richard Heidrich, was made commander of I Parachute Corps, while the man who assumed command of his division was Oberst Karl-Lothar Schulz. The latter distinguished himself at Anzio and during the withdrawal into northern Italy, adding the Oakleaves and Swords to his Knight's Cross. Both the 1st and 4th Parachute Divisions were given additional firepower during this period, the 1st receiving the 1st Parachute Mortar Battalion and the 4th receiving the 4th Parachute Mortar Battalion.*

Air Force, the offensive rapidly gained ground and Allied forces had penetrated the Gothic Line near the coastal town of Pesaro by 30 August. However, Kesselring soon plugged the breach with the 26th Panzer, 29th Panzergrenadier and 356th Infantry Divisions. The seemingly endless rivers and ridges, plus bad weather, meant Axis units had stalled Eighth Army forces short of their Rimini and Romagna Plain objectives by 3 September.

Clark planned to open his phase of Operation "Olive" on 10 September 1944 with an assault by the two corps under his command. As expected, the Germans began withdrawing to the Gothic Line several days before the advance and initial resistance was light. However, as the advancing forces reached the mountains, the intensity of the fighting increased. The Eighth Army's attack in the east had succeeded in diverting most enemy units away from the Futa Pass and Il Giogo Pass areas, except for three regiments of I Parachute Corps' 4th Parachute Division. In the west only the 362nd and 65th Infantry Divisions faced the US IV Corps.

The terrain of mountain peaks, streams, deep valleys and ridges meant small-unit actions predominated, and the paras put up their usual dogged resistance. The Fallschirmjäger had heavily fortified the Futa Pass, but were surprised by the US attacks against the Il Giogo Pass and nearby Monticelli Ridge and Monte Altuzzo. By 18 September, after heavy fighting, I Parachute Corps withdrew to the next set of ridges to establish another defence line. Encouraged at having breached the Gothic Line in at least one sector the Americans continued their offensive, and in response the paras defended each position in a series of intense small-unit actions.

As the Fifth Army continued its offensive, the British Eighth Army resumed Operation "Olive" on 12 September. With overwhelming superiority in tanks,

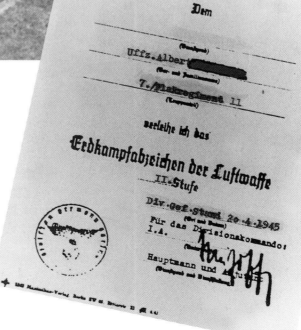

Left: *On parade in Italy. The man nearest the camera is wearing the Spanish Cross award, indicating service with the German Condor Legion in Spain during the Civil War. He is also wearing the second model, front-lacing Fallschirmjäger jump boots, which were introduced shortly after the outbreak of war in 1939. The boots were of conventional design, with leather soles and heels, which were usually studded. The original jump boots had side lacing and were designed to give additional support to the wearer's ankles. They were manufactured from both black leather and from dark brown leather, with the soles and heels being made of moulded rubber with a chevron patterning. There were 12 lace holes to each boot, which reached to just below mid-calf level. The side-lacing boots were worn up to and including the Battle of Crete in 1941, and thereafter became scarce as stocks were exhausted.*

Right: *Citation for the Luftwaffe Ground Assault Badge shown at the top of page 125. Awarded to a man called Unteroffizier Hauser (who subsequently masked his name on the document to maintain his anonymity), 2nd Flak Regiment, he later went on to win the "50" assaults badge. It is interesting to note that unlike the army numbered assault badges, which were in two distinct designs (one for 25 and 50, the other for 75 and 100 ground assault actions), the Luftwaffe badges were identical for all grades. By the later stages of the war many Luftwaffe units were fighting alongside army and Waffen-SS formations. This award, for example, is dated 20 April 1945.*

Right: *The Ground Assault Badge 25. The central, upper portion of the wreath is made up of clouds, with a lightning bolt striking the ground. The flying Luftwaffe eagle is incorporated across the wreath and over the clouds. The numbers in the box at the base of the badge represent the number of ground engagements with which the recipient was credited. From either side of the box emanate the tip of an oakleaf over a single leaf. From these, on either side, are seven fans of three oakleaves reducing slightly in width until they meet at the apex, tip to tip. Members of parachute units and assault gun units were authorised to receive the numbered badges.*

Left: *An unidentified Luftwaffe member wearing the Ground Assault Badge. The badge was instituted on 31 March 1942 to reward members of the Luftwaffe who were engaged in military operations in support of the German Army. If an army award badge, such as the General Assault Badge, Infantry Assault Badge or Tank Assault Badge, had been awarded previously to the institution of this badge, it was to be exchanged for this badge. The criteria for the award were as follows: being involved in three engagements on different days; being wounded in one of the actions for which this badge could have been awarded; to have been awarded a decoration in one of these actions; and a Luftwaffe member killed during an action was automatically awarded the badge. Members of parachute units and assault gun units were also authorised to receive the badge provided they fulfilled the same qualifications.*

aircraft and troops, the British V and Canadian I Corps smashed through defence lines manned by the 29th Panzergrenadier and 1st Parachute Divisions to capture Rimini, the gateway to the Romagna Plain, on 21 September. In the face of stubborn resistance, heavy rain and mud, the Eighth Army continued its attack and began a three-month operation called the "battle of the rivers". Against adverse weather conditions and fanatical resistance, the Eighth Army made only slow progress.

The weather deteriorates

Poor weather was also having an affect on Clark's progress, that and German resistance. Fog and mist drastically decreased visibility, and torrential rains swelled streams, washed out bridges and created quagmires that made troop and supply movements over mountain trails treacherous. Between 5–9 October, for example, Fifth Army units advanced only 4.8km (three miles) for the loss of 1400 casualties. The Germans were paying a high price for their tenacity, though, especially when they mounted counterattacks. Kesselring therefore ordered his subordinates to conserve their manpower by digging in and conducting a defence in depth rather than trying to retake lost mountain tops (he knew that if the Americans advanced out of the Apennines and entered the Po Valley before winter, Axis forces in Italy would be doomed).

A vicious battle was fought on the Livergnano Escarpment, a steep east-west line of solitary mountain peaks constituting the enemy's strongest natural position in the northern Apennines. The US II Corps' assault began on 10 October. The 85th Division led the primary attack against Monte delle Formiche in the centre of the escarpment, while the 91st and 88th Divisions maintained pressure on the enemy's flanks. The defending units were the 4th

Above: *Paratroopers haul Teller mines to the front. This type of antitank mine consisted of a flat cylinder of metal with a sprung lid, which was set off by pressure from above. The charge was usually TNT or Amatol, and the mines were laid 50.8–101.6mm (2–4in) below the ground. The Germans also developed a variety of highly effective antipersonnel mines, which gave a shrapnel burst when tripped.*

Parachute, 94th, 362nd and 65th Infantry Divisions. Supported by air strikes, the 85th Division succeeded in taking Monte delle Formiche that day, while the 91st Division outflanked the Livergnano Escarpment from the west, forcing the Axis units in the area to withdraw on 13 October. However, Axis resistance, rugged terrain and poor weather halted II Corps' advance 16km (10 miles) south of Bologna.

The Allies run out of steam

Kesselring's staff were urging him to retreat to the more defendable Alps. Hitler, however, facing Red Army gains on the Eastern Front and Allied successes in northwest Europe, ordered the field marshal to hold his current positions. As far as the Fallschirmjäger were concerned it was business as usual, as the Americans battled their way from mountain to mountain, and Polish, Canadian, Indian and British troops of the Eighth Army attacked north of Rimini on 15 October in a continuation of the "battle of the rivers". However, not even the Allies could sustain high-intensity operations indefinitely. Between 10 September and 26 October, for example, the US II Corps' four divisions had suffered over 15,000 casualties, and during the same period Eighth Army casualties neared 14,000 men.

In early January 1945 the Allies in Italy ceased large-scale military operations. In addition to the bad weather, five Eighth Army divisions and one corps headquarters had been moved to northwest Europe and Greece, further diminishing Allied capabilities in Italy. Alexander, Clark, Truscott and McCreery, therefore, agreed to go on the defensive and use the winter months to prepare for new offensive operations, scheduled to begin on 1 April 1945. Despite two months of planning and limited offensives, Allied units came to rest on a winter line that had changed very little since late October 1944. The approaching spring would bring a fresh effort by the Fifteenth Army Group as it prepared to renew the offensive in a campaign to take it into the Po Valley. Despite being inferior in manpower, aircraft, armour and artillery, the Germans had displayed remarkable courage and resilience.

As 1945 opened the Allies still faced an organised and determined foe in Italy consisting of 24 German and five Italian fascist divisions. Among the best

Above: *Close-up of a camouflaged paratrooper helmet. It was designed to withstand the hard blows encountered during a heavy landing. Its shape was also intended to prevent it from becoming entangled in parachute rigging or harness lines. The special neck and chin straps were anchored to the helmet at the rear and sides.*

Left: *The Fallschirmjäger on the right with his back to the camera carries one of the weapons specially developed for the German airborne arm: the Rheinmetall-designed 7.92mm Fallschirmjägergewehr 42 automatic rifle. The curiously contoured butt contained a buffer spring assembly to help reduce recoil.*

were those in the German Tenth Army's I Parachute Corps. The Fallschirmjäger were by this time experienced veterans who belonged to relatively intact units. That said, they lacked vehicles, air support and were experiencing shortages of equipment. The first Axis defensive line, along the northern Apennines, protected Bologna and blocked entry into the east-west Po Valley, about 80km (50 miles) farther north. The second defence line was anchored along the River Po, which from its source in northwestern Italy meanders east to the Adriatic Sea. The third line, in the Alpine foothills, extended east and west of Lake Garda. Dubbed the Adige Line, after the river of the same name, these defences were designed to cover a last-ditch Axis withdrawal into northeast Italy and Austria.

The final push

The last Allied offensive in Italy opened on 5 April 1945. On the Adriatic coast, the 26th Panzer, 98th Infantry, 362nd Infantry, 4th Parachute and 42nd Jäger Divisions battled units of the Eighth Army. The Argenta Gap fell on 18 April, which threatened to turn the entire Axis flank.

In the US sector, during the afternoon of 15 April, over 760 heavy bombers of the Mediterranean Allied Strategic Air Force pounded positions held by the 65th Division and 8th Mountain Division of XIV Panzer Corps and the 1st Parachute and 305th Infantry Divisions of I Parachute Corps. The Germans continued to fight, but wavered in the face of a massive ground and aerial onslaught. By 18 April, as Axis defences cracked, the bulk of the US Fifth Army passed west of Bologna. Two days later both the Fifth and Eighth Armies

Above: *Demolitions on the Gothic Line to stall the Allied advance. In September 1944, three regiments of the 4th Parachute Division were defending the Futa and Il Giogo Passes when attacked by the US 91st and 85th Divisions. Six days of intense fighting between 12–18 September resulted in the Americans seizing the Il Giogo Pass, Monticelli Ridge and Monte Altuzzo. The Americans lost 2730 men, though, and only forced the Fallschirmjäger from the Il Giogo Pass by deploying overwhelming firepower.*

Left: *These men are probably members of the 4th Parachute Division. Two types of ammunition carriers can be seen in this photograph. The soldier on the left wears the Fallschirmjäger rifle ammunition bandolier, while his companion on the right has pouches for submachine gun magazines. The division was heavily engaged in the Florence area in November 1944, where it tried to repel heavy Allied attacks. The fighting earned many Fallschirmjäger gallantry awards, such as Hauptmann Erich Beine, commander of the 3rd Battalion, 12th Parachute Assault Regiment, who won a Knight's Cross. Another Knight's Cross winner was Feldwebel Rudolf Donth, 4th Parachute Regiment, 1st Parachute Division, who helped to repulse three enemy tank attacks in the Savio area, personally knocking out six tanks in the last attack. He later defeated a British battalion attack near Monte Castellero.*

Above: *Typical Fallschirmjäger appearance during the latter stages of the Italian campaign: sloppily dressed but sporting massive firepower. The weapon carried over the shoulder of the soldier in the centre is the MG 42, one of the finest machine guns ever made. With a cyclic rate of fire of 1200–1500 rounds per minute, the MG 42 was able to lay down heavy fire even using short bursts. Allied soldiers came to fear its "ripping sheet" sound, while German soldiers couldn't get enough of the weapon. Some 414,964 were produced in total, with the Luftwaffe taking delivery of 4014. The beauty of the MG 42 was that it was well made and a lot of thought had gone into its design, especially materials and features such as easy barrel changes. The result was a weapon that was efficient and reliable under the most arduous weather conditions. The MG 42 had a muzzle velocity of 822mps (2737fps) and a range of 1000m (3300ft).*

launched high-speed armoured advances from the Apennine foothills towards the River Po crossings. It was now a race between Allied and Axis forces to reach the river first and the Alpine foothills beyond.

A hopeless task

The 1st and 4th Parachute Divisions desperately tried to buy time for small detachments of their comrades to escape. But the Allied onslaught swept aside their defences and annihilated Axis rearguard detachments. Now that the Allies were in the open their overwhelming airpower, which the mountain fighting had negated to a certain extent, could add massive support to ground forces. The rapid advance had created many pockets of Axis soldiers, and special task forces had to be created to mop them up. Eventually over 100,000 Axis troops were forced to surrender in the areas south of the river.

By 24 April the entire Fifth Army front had reached the Po, while to the east Eighth Army units were within a few miles of the River Po by nightfall on 23 April. The Germans had nothing left to stop the Allies crossing the river. The capture of Verona on 26 April brought the Allies up to the final Axis defensive line in Italy: the Adige Line. Though imposing, the Germans now lacked the materiel and manpower to organise a cohesive barrier. Indeed, by this time most Axis units had disintegrated into small groups of harried soldiers retreating as best they could in the face of intense Allied pressure.

Resistance was very light now as the Allies advanced, and the towns of Parma, Fidenza and Piacenza were captured in quick succession. Tens of thousands of Axis prisoners now fell into Allied hands, and the ragged survivors of the battered 1st and 4th Parachute Divisions surrendered at the beginning of May. On the afternoon of 3 May 1945, Lieutenant-General Fridolin von Senger und Etterlin, Vietinghoff's representative, formally surrendered the remaining Axis forces in Italy.

Above: *A heavily armed Fallschirmjäger patrol in Normandy. The belts of ammunition are for the MG 42 machine gun, which employed 50- or 250-round belts of 7.92mm rounds.*

CAMPAIGN IN THE WEST, 1944–45

In the face of massive Allied firepower and aerial superiority, the parachute divisions in the West fought valiantly to try to contain the Normandy bridgehead, and then hold the borders of the Third Reich itself. But, along with other German divisions, the Fallschirmjäger were exhausted by relentless combat and a deluge of enemy manpower and resources.

Left: *In the Bocage, July 1944. This photograph affords a good view of the FG 42 automatic rifle. Around 7000 were produced during the war. The trigger mechanism involved a closed bolt for single-shot fire, while the bolt remained open between bursts to cool the barrel and breech.*

On 3 November 1943, Hitler issued his Directive No 51 for the defence of occupied France. It began: "For the last two and one-half years the bitter and costly struggle against Bolshevism has made the utmost demands upon the bulk of our military resources and energies. This commitment was in keeping with the seriousness of the danger, and the overall situation. The situation has since changed. The threat from the East remains, but an even greater danger looms in the West: the Anglo-American landing! In the East, the vastness of the space will, as a last resort, permit a loss of territory even on a major scale, without suffering a mortal blow to Germany's chance for survival. Not so in the West! If the enemy here succeeds in penetrating our defences on a wide front, consequences of staggering proportions will follow within a short time." The directive went on to detail the proposed buildup of forces in the West to meet the invasion. Though fanciful in parts, it contained a statement that was to come all too true for many German formations: "other available personnel are to be organised into battalions of replacements and equipped with the available weapons, so that the anticipated heavy losses can quickly be replaced."

The German order of battle

Despite the Führer's orders, the German Army in the West on the eve of Operation "Overlord", the Allied invasion of Normandy, was considerably weaker than planned in terms of equipment, quality and numbers. In June 1944 the commander of the Western Theatre, Field Marshal Gerd von Rundstedt, had 58 combat divisions divided between four armies. These armies were the First (commanded by General Joachim Lemelsen) holding the Atlantic coast of France, the Seventh (commanded by General Friedrich Dollmann) occupying Brittany and most of Normandy, the Fifteenth (commanded by General Hans von Salmuth) between Le Havre and Flushing, and the Nineteenth (commanded by General Georg von Sodenstern) deployed along the French Mediterranean coast. The Fifteenth and Seventh Armies were grouped under Army Group B, commanded by Field Marshal Erwin Rommel. The First and Nineteenth Armies were grouped under Army Group G, commanded by Generaloberst Johannes Blaskowitz.

Because of units being stripped of troops and hardware for service on the Eastern Front, plus the policy of allocating the best weapons and equipment to

Below: *General Kurt Student reviews some of his men in France in 1944. Throughout 1943 and 1944 the German airborne arm was reorganised and expanded, and by the summer of 1944 he had 30,000 trained parachutists. Units were also rebuilt as a result of losses suffered in Italy and on the Eastern Front. The 2nd Parachute Division was formed in February 1943 in France, being established around the 2nd Parachute Regiment and a battalion from the 1st Parachute Artillery Regiment. Its first commander was General Bernhard Ramcke. The 3rd Parachute Division was formed in Reims in late 1943. Commanded by Generalmajor Richard Schimpf, its young volunteers were built around a cadre of battle-hardened veterans. The 5th Parachute Division, commanded by Generalleutnant Gustav Wilke, was also formed in Reims, while the 6th Parachute Division, commanded by Generalleutnant Rüdiger von Heyking, was formed in Amiens.*

the same theatre first, many German infantry, panzer and panzergrenadier divisions in the West immediately prior to the D-Day landings were understrength and equipped with second-rate captured tanks. This meant that the Fallschirmjäger divisions in the West were among Rundstedt's best units when the Allies landed. In fact, the Luftwaffe had been carrying out a restructuring of its parachute divisions since November 1943 (administratively under the Luftwaffe, in the field by this stage of the war parachute units were always tactically controlled by the army) as a result of the severe losses suffered in Italy and on the

Above: *Route marches, the bane of a soldier's life. This group of paras in France in early 1944 has a mix of army and airborne helmets, and not all are shouldering rifles. They are wearing splinter-pattern camouflage jump smocks and front-lacing jump boots. In 1942 a number of jump schools had been set up in France, at Chateaudun, Dreux, Lyon, Orange and Toyes.*

Left: *Young Fallschirmjäger recruits in France. By the middle of 1944 the programme of strengthening the parachute divisions had been a great success in terms of manpower. The 3rd Parachute Division, for example, was fully staffed and trained by the beginning of June. However, there were a number of problems with hardware: the division was suffering a 30 percent shortfall in weapons, most noticeably in machine guns and antitank weapons; it had only enough ammunition for six days of combat; and it possessed only 40 percent of its truck allocation (and hardly any fuel for those it did have). The 5th Parachute Division was in a slightly better position, suffering only a five percent shortfall in weapons and equipment. However, it had a 70 percent shortfall in vehicles and many of its recruits had not finished their parachute training by D-Day.*

Eastern Front. The result was the formation of I Parachute Corps in Italy and II Parachute Corps, which on 26 April 1944 was transferred to Brittany to reinforce local defence forces in the area. In May the corps was made up of the following units: the 3rd Parachute Division (headquarters at Huelgoal, Brittany), 5th Parachute Division (headquarters at Rennes, Brittany), and 2nd Parachute Division (this much-weakened unit was at Köln-Wahn in Germany undergoing rest and refitting). In addition, the 6th Parachute Regiment under Major Freiherr von der Heydte was in Normandy in the Lessay-Mont Castre-Carentan area. Briefly attached to the 2nd Parachute Division, this unit was the only Fallschirmjäger formation in Normandy in May 1944.

Left: *Though this photograph perhaps paints a too rosy picture of relations between German troops and French civilians, often the relationship between the two was amicable. The young paratroopers found service in France before D-Day very agreeable, and those units deployed to rural areas in the main did not suffer from partisan activities. Gefreiter Pollman, who served in a pioneer battalion, was a typical example: "Quartered at Marcilly-sur-Eure with my company, I was transferred to the headquarters of Ivry-la-Bataille. My group was tasked with equipment servicing and maintenance. At our disposal were a small cottage and a large shed. The field latrines were located by a small brook."*

Above: *A Fallschirmjäger flak unit pillages milk from a member of the local population! Most German flak artillery was operated by the Luftwaffe, and by the end of the war no less than 30 flak divisions, plus numerous flak brigades, had been formed. Antiaircraft defences in Normandy would prove almost useless against what the German military called the Materialschlacht: the seemingly unending streams of Allied aircraft that delivered crippling attacks from above. Between 9 February 1944 and D-Day, for example, the US Ninth Army Air Force and the Second Tactical Air Force of the RAF committed a total of 5677 aircraft against German targets in France to prepare the ground for the invasion.*

The formation of the two parachute corps was only one part of a grand scheme devised by Göring for the formation of two parachute armies with a total strength of 100,000 men. The plan was approved by Hitler. Despite the fact that the days of large airborne operations were over, the various parachute units could still be classed as élites. Composed entirely of young volunteers from the draft (the average age of enlisted men in the 6th Parachute Regiment, for example, was 17 and a half), they were well armed and highly motivated. By May 1944, for example, the strength of the 3rd Parachute Division stood at 17,420 men, having been only formed in Reims in October 1943. Another factor that made the para units so potent, especially in defence, was that they usually had a higher percentage of support weapons than infantry divisions. The rifle companies of the 6th Parachute Regiment, for example, had twice as many light machine guns as infantry rifle division companies.

II Parachute Corps, commanded by General Eugen Meindl, was part of the Seventh Army, and in April Hitler had begun to show an interest in Normandy as a potential invasion site. In response to this, the Seventh Army had moved the 6th Parachute Regiment to the Lessay-Periers area, where it was subordinated to the 91st Division. Its immediate mission was defence against airborne landings.

On 6 June 1944, the Western Allies launched the greatest amphibious operation in history. The statistics for the invasion force were staggering:

50,000 men for the initial assault; over two million men to be shipped to France in all, comprising a total of 39 divisions; 139 major warships used in the assault, with a further 221 smaller combat vessels; over 1000 minesweepers and auxiliary vessels; 4000 landing craft; 805 merchant ships; 59 blockships; 300 miscellaneous small craft; and 11,000 aircraft, including fighters, bombers, transports and gliders. In addition, the invasion force had the support of over 100,000 members of the French Resistance.

D-Day, the Allied invasion of Normandy, codenamed Operation "Overlord", began with the assault of three airborne divisions – the US 82nd and 101st on the right flank of the American forces, and the British 6th Airborne on the left flank of the British – while seaborne forces landed on five beaches. The main components of the invasion force, grouped under the umbrella of General Bernard Montgomery's Twenty-First Army Group, were the British Second Army under General Miles Dempsey and the US First Army under General Omar Bradley. Utah Beach was the target of the US 4th Infantry Division (part of the US VII Corps); Omaha Beach was the target of the US 1st Infantry Division (part of the US V Corps); Gold Beach was the landing site of the British 50th Infantry Division (part of the British XXX Corps); Juno was the target for the Canadian 3rd Infantry Division (part of the British I Corps); and the British 3rd Infantry Division was tasked with seizing Sword Beach (also part of the British I Corps).

Below: *Training to use the 37mm Pak 35/36 antitank gun in France. By 1944 this weapon, which had proved ineffective against some British and French tanks in 1940, was almost useless against Allied tanks about to invade Normandy. The gun had a stay of execution with the introduction into service of two new rounds that enhanced its performance. The first was the 37mm Panzergranate 40 (PzGr 40) tungsten-carbide round. Introduced in late 1940, it could penetrate up to 65mm (2.6in) of vertical armour. The second was the 37mm Stielgranate 41 stick bomb. Introduced in 1941, it was fitted over the muzzle of the gun and fired by means of a blank cartridge in the breech. Despite these improvements, the gun was still derisively known as the "door knocker".*

Above: *A Fallschirmjäger 20mm Flakvierling 38 four-barrelled, light antiaircraft gun. Entering service in 1940, it operated with each parachute division's antiaircraft battalion. Its four barrels could fire up to 1800 rounds a minute, making it deadly for low-flying aircraft, though it was also effective against ground targets. Each gun had a muzzle velocity of 900mps (2951fps) and a maximum ceiling of 2200m (7221ft). This photograph was taken on the eve of D-Day. At this time the parachute divisions were staffed by divisional, regimental and battalion commanders who had more combat experience than their Allied opponents. They also had a major advantage at the lower levels: their NCOs were of a very high quality who would not hesitate to assume responsibility or use initiative as the situation demanded.*

The initial parachute and seaborne landings had mixed results: on Utah resistance was light and the troops were off the beach by 12:00 hours; on Omaha the lack of specialised armour meant the Germans could pin down the troops on the beach, with great slaughter; on Gold and Juno the specialised armour of the British and Canadians allowed the troops to get off the beaches quickly, and by the afternoon they were probing inland towards Bayeux and Caen; and on Sword the troops were able to link up with airborne units farther inland. The general Allied strategy was to capture Cherbourg for use as a port, prior to advancing south into Brittany and east across the River Seine. By the end of the day 155,000 Allied troops had been landed, backed up by massive aerial superiority and naval gunfire support.

The initial German response

The Germans were in a dilemma with regard to the landings, as they were unsure whether they were secondary to the main effort in the Pas de Calais. Hitler for one believed so, and he refused to release the mobile reserves from Panzer Group West until late in the afternoon of 6 June. In addition, von Rundstedt refused to allow two panzer divisions located north of the Seine to be switched to Normandy. In a sense this was largely irrelevant, for even when the mobile reserves were deployed Allied air power meant movement took longer than anticipated and units were committed to the battle piecemeal. This meant that effective counterattacks against the beachhead could not be mounted, and the panzer units consequently found themselves in an infantry support role.

On 6 June itself II Parachute Corps was ordered to Normandy immediately to repel a reported Allied airborne drop near Coutances. When this proved untrue, the corps was ordered to mount a counterattack in the area of St. Lô, together with the 352nd Infantry Division and the 17th SS Panzergrenadier Division *Götz von Berlichingen*, which was at the time some distance away. At this time II Parachute Corps was at Les Cheris, 10km (six miles) southeast of Avranches, and under the tactical command of LXXXIV Corps. The condition of the various corps units was as follows: the 3rd Parachute Division was positioned midway between Quimper and Brest; the 5th Parachute Division was not ready for combat, and so only its 15th Parachute Regiment was transferred to the front.

In response to the invasion, Fallschirmjäger units were ordered to seize strategic locations that had not yet been taken by US forces. Von der Heydte ordered his 2nd Battalion to take St. Marie-Eglise, the 1st Battalion to take St. Marie du Mont and the 3rd Battalion to take Carentan. In fact, the 6th

Below: *Fighting on the Normandy Front in June 1944. On D-Day the only Fallschirmjäger unit in the area was von der Heydte's 6th Parachute Regiment, part of the 2nd Parachute Division. When the invasion took place it immediately moved to the Carentan area. Gefreiter Primetzhofer, 13th Company, was one of its members, and commented on "the heavy shelling of the Allied warships which opened up at around 5am. According to my estimates, the rolling, long-range fire lasted 15 hours, after which I thought that I was the only survivor of my unit. Fortunately, this was not the case."*

Right: *A Kattenkrad (motorcycle tractor) in Normandy. These vehicles, used for towing equipment, were usually attached to divisional motorcycle companies. In Normandy they were scarce among the parachute divisions, all of which suffered acute shortages of vehicles throughout the campaign.*

Below: *The FG 42 was the product of a Fallschirmjäger request for a cross between an automatic rifle and a light machine gun. The weapon had a number of faults: the complex but inefficient muzzle brake did not eliminate flash, the bipod was too flimsy for prolonged firing, and the lightweight barrel soon overheated during continuous firing.*

Parachute Regiment was one of the first German units to engage Allied forces in Normandy, when it was involved in heavy fighting against the US 1st Infantry Division around Carentan. The 1st Battalion was all but wiped out and the other two battalions had to fight desperately to hold on to the town. With the Americans controlling all the surrounding roads and the air, the paras received just one airdrop of ammunition to enable them to break out of the town. On 12 June, following heavy losses and the refusal of the 17th SS Panzergrenadier Division to provide reinforcements, the 6th Parachute Regiment was withdrawn and redeployed to the Vire sector to fight under the 2nd SS Panzer Division *Das Reich*.

Meanwhile, the 2nd Parachute Division under General Bernhard Ramcke had been ordered to hold Brittany and had travelled from Germany by rail. The journey was long and hazardous, being frequently interrupted by Allied air

Left: *The two photographs on this page show a Fallschirmjäger squad resting on the Normandy Front. This particular image shows the men watching Allied aircraft passing overhead. At this time Luftflotte III was totally swamped, and even when German aircraft managed to penetrate to the bridgehead they were shot to pieces by the plethora of Allied fighters.*

strikes and partisan attacks. The first elements of the division reach Brittany on 19 June, but the rest did not join them until July. This area was relatively calm, which gave the division time to work up those units manned by inexperienced replacements. It was the lull before the storm, for by 12 June alone the Allies had 326,547 men ashore in Normandy. Montgomery was determined to make his breakout attempt with the US First Army on the right flank, pivoting around the British Second Army at Caen. The Americans launched their offensive to cut off the port of Cherbourg, which fell to the US VII Corps under Lieutenant-General J. Lawton Collins on 29 June. For the Americans and Germans, and especially the Fallschirmjäger, the Normandy campaign was about to enter its bloodiest phase.

Below: *Of interest in this photograph is the captured British Bren Gun being held by the para in the bottom left-hand corner of the image. At this time units were experiencing problems getting reinforcements and supplies from rear areas because of enemy air attacks. As a result, most movement had to be made during the hours of darkness.*

Following the fall of Cherbourg, the US First Army sought to win the line Coutances-Marigny-St. Lô, which would allow it to launch an offensive south and east to break out of Normandy. Opposed to the Americans were the paras of II Parachute Corps. Though outgunned and outnumbered, the Germans were greatly aided by the terrain of the so-called Bocage. A US Army report describes it thus: "But the Germans' greatest advantage lay in the hedgerows which crisscrossed the country everywhere, hampering offensive action and

Right: *A wounded paratrooper in Normandy. During June the US First Army took Cherbourg and cleared most of the Cotentin Peninsula and had then turned south. German resistance had been centred around Carentan and Caen (it would take the British until 13 July to take the latter). As the British advanced towards Caen, the US First Army held a line from Caumont to Carentan and west across the peninsula. Supplies and reinforcements were pouring into the beachhead to prepare for an offensive to break out of the Normandy pocket. The offensive that later became known as the "Battle of the Hedgerows" around St. Lô was designed to gain room and jump-off positions for that offensive. Opposing the Americans was the Seventh Army, commanded by SS-Lieutenant-General Paul Hausser, specifically the units of LXXXIV and II Parachute Corps.*

limiting the use of tanks. An aerial photograph of a typical section of Normandy shows more than 3900 hedged enclosures in an area of less than eight square miles. Growing out of massive embankments that formed dikes up to 10 feet high, often flanked by drainage ditches or sunken roads, the hedges lent themselves easily to skillful organization of dug-in emplacements and concealed strongpoints." St. Lô was the hub of a road network that spread in every direction, and thus had to be taken.

The US attack began on 3 July, and a combination of the terrain and fanatical German resistance made the going slow and costly in terms of lives. The close-quarter nature of the fighting largely negated Allied air power, so that the "Battle of the Hedgerows" became a multitude of small-scale actions. German troops did not try to form a continuous line, but rather relied on a number of strongpoints that could support each other by interlocking fields of fire. In addition to defending, the paras also launched effective counterattacks. On 11

Above: *Mortars of the 3rd Parachute Division in Normandy, mid-July 1944. At this time the division comprised three regiments of three battalions each, with a mortar, antitank and engineer company within each regiment. Some regiments had heavy 120mm mortars whereas others had 100mm models and even Nebelwerfer (multi-barrelled mortars). The division had only one battalion of light artillery, but its antiaircraft battalion boasted 12 88mm guns. On 22 May 1944 the division had mustered 17,420 men.*

Above: *A machine-gun team takes up position, mid-1944. The marshy lands south and southwest of Carentan had been partly flooded by the Germans to aid their defences, and the rains that fell in the area in June and July further impeded the Allied advance. The wet conditions also aided the defence at St. Lô, around which was a network of poor roads, sunken lanes and farm tracks, all of which became very muddy very quickly.*

July, for example, the commander of the US 1st Battalion, 115th Infantry Regiment, reported a "beautifully executed and planned" attack by the 1st Battalion, 9th Parachute Regiment (part of the 3rd Parachute Division). The paras laid down a barrage of mortar and artillery fire and then followed at a distance of 46m (150ft). Achieving almost complete surprise, the 115th's outposts were immediately overrun. However, the attack was held and the paras retreated. The US battalion had lost 100 men, but so had the paras, and these were losses the Germans could ill afford. Indeed, the Americans actually welcome these attacks, as a US soldier who fought in the Bocage states: "German counterattacks in the hedgerows failed largely for the same reasons our own advance was slowed. Any attack quickly loses its momentum, and then because of our artillery and fighter bombers the Germans would suffer disastrous loss.

Right: *A paratrooper in the Bocage awaits the US attack in his foxhole, stick grenade at the ready. The attack of the US XIX Corps began on 3 July in heavy rain. As soon as it started Seventh Army was asking Field Marshal Günther von Kluge, the new overall commander in the West, for reinforcements to be sent to it from Brittany.*

In fact, we found that generally the best way to beat the Germans was to get them to counterattack – provided we had prepared to meet them."

The fall of Hill 192

Gradually the Americans fought their way forward, suffering heavy losses in the process, until they were on the outskirts of St. Lô itself. The key to the town was Hill 192, a commanding height 4.8km (three miles) to the east. The defence of this feature was initially in the hands of the 3rd Battalion, 9th Parachute Regiment, and the 1st Battalion, 5th Parachute Regiment. Following a heavy artillery barrage, the US attack began at 06:00 hours on 11 July. Resistance was its usual fanatical self, and soon the Germans were feeding in new units to hold their positions: the 12th Parachute Gun Brigade, 3rd Parachute Reconnaissance Company and 3rd Parachute Engineer Battalion. However, all the Fallschirmjäger units were badly mauled in the fighting, and by the next day the 3rd Parachute Division was desperately scraping together its last reserves to form a new defence line south of the St. Lô-Bayeux highway.

Above: *The mighty "88" in the Bocage. The German 88mm antiaircraft gun was discovered to be ideal for knocking out enemy tanks, having a high muzzle velocity – 820–840mps (2733–2754fps) – and a ceiling/range of 10,600m (34,788ft). It could knock out any Allied tank in service, and was also a potent antipersonnel weapon when firing fused shells to produce air-burst. The gun was usually mounted on a two-wheeled field carriage as the 88mm Pak 43/41. Note how the gun is heavily camouflaged as a defence against air attack by the enemy.*

The nature of the fighting for the hill is described by a para who fought there, and shows that even élite troops have their mental and physical limits: "Carried my machine gun through the enemy lines into a slightly more protected defile and crept back again with another fellow to get the wounded. On our way back we were covered again with terrific artillery fire. We were just lying in an open area. Every moment I expected deadly shrapnel. At that moment I lost my nerve. The others acted just like me. When one hears for hours the whining, whistling and bursting of shells and the moaning and groaning of the wounded, one does not feel too well. Our company had only 30 men left (out of 170)." In three days of fighting the 3rd Parachute Division had lost 4064 men. By 14 July II Parachute Corps had no reserves left, and Meindl informed Rommel that, as he had received no replacements, he could not hold his present positions. But hold the paras did, at least until 27 July when US forces finally broke through at St. Lô. The "Battle of the Hedgerows" cost the US First Army 11,000 dead, wounded and missing between 7–22 July.

The Normandy Front collapse

On 25 July US forces began their breakout from Normandy. The newly arrived Third Army under General George S. Patton advanced west into Brittany, while Montgomery's Twenty-First Army Group also broke out from Normandy. The German Seventh Army was reeling, and much of it was destroyed around Falaise, in the so-called "Falaise Pocket". Ramcke's 2nd Parachute Division was involved in the defence of Brest, fighting the US VIII Corps as it advanced to invest the port. The Americans lost 4000 men, but the Fallschirmjäger also suffered heavy

Below: *Keeping watch for the Americans. For US units fighting in the Bocage, combat was close-quarter and confusing. A report dated 9 July from the US 823rd Tank Destroyer Battalion stated: "There were lots of small-arms fire, shelling and mortar fire blanketed the area, everybody fired in every direction, rumours flooded the air, and when infantry units withdrew in disorder leaving some guns exposed, it became necessary to withdraw to successive positions. The exact movements of each platoon is at present obscured in the confusion of battle."*

casualties. Ramcke was ordered to send a battle group to support the weakened 5th Parachute Division, but on the way it was badly mauled by an American armoured column before reaching St. Malo. Brest and the majority of the 2nd Parachute Division fell into US hands on 20 September 1944.

What was left of II Parachute Corps was sent to Cologne after Falaise for rest and refitting, while von der Heydte's 6th Parachute Regiment (which had lost a staggering 3000 men killed or missing since 6 June) was moved to Guestrow-Mecklenburg to form the cadre of a new regiment. German forces in France had in the meantime lost cohesion and were retreating east in disorder. The Allies secured their first crossing over the River Seine on 19 August, and six days later they entered Paris. Allied forces had also landed in southern France on 15 August, and the US Seventh and French First Armies were advancing rapidly north. The shattered German armies were unable to halt the

Below: *The crew of a US jeep takes cover as it comes under enemy mortar fire near St. Lô. During the battle for the town the Fallschirmjäger held the tactically important Hill 192 nearby, which gave them excellent observation over the whole countryside from the River Vire to Caumont, including all the approaches to St. Lô. The hill's slopes were covered by intricate patterns of hedgerowed fields and orchards. Attacks were costly: two assaults by the US 2nd Division in mid-July resulted in 1253 casualties and no ground won.*

Right: *Living in the ground became second nature for Fallschirmjäger in the Bocage. US artillery expended vast amounts of ammunition trying to force a way through at St. Lô. On 9 July, for example, the 30th Division's seven artillery battalions fired 5000 rounds of 105mm shells and 4000 rounds of 155mm ammunition.*

Below: *An MG 42 machine gunner in the Bocage. German mortar and machine-gun fire was very effective in the hedgerows. One strongpoint near the hamlet of Cloville was dubbed "Kraut Corner" by the Americans. It took an entire company one hour to destroy it, the last three paras being buried alive by a tank.*

Allies, as Brussels and Lyons fell on 3 September. General Dwight Eisenhower, supreme Allied commander, ordered that Montgomery was to pursue the German armies into the Ruhr while Bradley was to move into the Saarland. As Allied patrols crossed the German border near Luxembourg on 11 September, it appeared that the Allies would be in Berlin by the end of the year. However, fuel shortages resulted in the advance grinding to a halt all along the front. The Germans had a breathing space.

The First Parachute Army was initially used as a training command attached to Army Group D in France (the army grew out of XI Flieger Corps, being reorganised as the First Parachute Army in January 1944). After the Allied breakthrough in France it took control of the defensive lines in Belgium and eastern Holland between Antwerp and Maastricht. Though called an army and commanded by General Student, it included Luftwaffe signallers, navigators, observers and other men who had no proper parachute training and no combat experience.

The 3rd and 5th Parachute Divisions were in a weakened state after their retreat from Normandy, and had left most of their heavy weapons behind in the general rout. The 5th was commanded by Generalmajor Heilmann and the 3rd

Below: *General Bernhard Ramcke surrenders Brest to the Americans, 19 September 1944. Patton's US Third Army broke through the Avranches Gap in early August, and over 50,000 Germans were captured in the Falaise Pocket, with another 10,000 being killed. Ramcke's 2nd Parachute Division saw little combat in Normandy, and in August and September participated in the defence of Brest. The majority of the division and its commander entered captivity when the port fell.*

by Generalmajor Walter Wadehn. In addition, von der Heydte's 6th Parachute Regiment was being reformed – just in time to meet Operation "Market Garden".

Montgomery had proposed to Eisenhower that the First Allied Airborne Army be used to turn the German flank by thrusting across the Lower Rhine in Holland. Three airborne drops would be made to secure bridges over canals in the Eindhoven area, the River Maas at Grave and River Waal at Nijmegen, and over the Rhine at Arnhem. On the ground, the British XXX Corps would advance into Holland and link up with the airborne forces.

"Market Garden" was launched on 17 September. It went well at first, with the US 82nd and 101st Airborne Divisions taking the Grave, Eindhoven and Nijmegen bridges. However, the Germans were quick to respond. There were two SS divisions refitting in the area – the 9th and 10th – plus army and

Fallschirmjäger units, and these quickly moved to isolate the Allied paratroopers. Fallschirmjäger formations were involved against the US 101st Airborne at Eindhoven and Grave, and von der Heydte's 6th Parachute Regiment also moved against their airborne opponents, though it was halted west of Eerde after heavy fighting on 23 September. Meindl's II Parachute Corps launched an attack southeast of Nijmegen, but it was beaten back by units of the US 82nd Airborne Division.

Preparations for the last offensive in the West

During this period of the war parachute units were forced to make long marches on foot, having inadequate transport. The 6th Parachute Regiment, for example, had to make a 60km (37.5-mile) march to reach its attack line near Boxtel. Allied air superiority made such marches hazardous, while the distances covered meant the troops attacked in an exhausted condition. Nevertheless, the paras did contribute to blunting "Market Garden", and de facto wrecked the last chance the Allies had of ending the war in 1944. In October 1944, the depleted II Parachute Corps was rebuilt once more to prepare for Germany's last great offensive in the West.

Hitler's counteroffensive in the West was designed to split British and US forces by thrusting towards Antwerp. Hitler launched Operation "Watch on the Rhine", his attempt to break though the US VIII Corps on the Ardennes Front,

Below: *Despite their losses in France, morale among the Fallschirmjäger in late 1944 was still high, as this photograph shows. Note the egg-shaped grenades in the belt of the para in the centre. The Eihandgranate 39 was a small blast grenade with a thin steel case. It weighed 340g (12oz), with 112g (4oz) of that being TNT filling. To operate it, a knob on top of the grenade was unscrewed and pulled, the grenade was thrown, and the charge exploded after a 4.5-second delay. Some 2,089,500 of these grenades were issued to the Luftwaffe in 1943–44.*

Above: *Three British airborne soldiers are escorted into captivity after the failure of "Market Garden", the dropping of three Allied divisions to seize bridges over the Meuse and Rhine to facilitate a thrust into Germany. The German reaction to the drops was swift and skilful. Student, as commander of the First Parachute Army, was on the spot to direct operations.*

reach the Meuse River and capture Antwerp, on 16 December 1944. The German units – 200,000 men in total – formed Army Group B under the overall command of Field Marshal Gerd von Rundstedt. This force comprised the Sixth SS Panzer Army, Fifth Panzer Army and Seventh Army. US forces amounted to 80,000 men. Surprise was total and the dense cloud and fog negated Allied air superiority. However, the Germans failed to immediately take the towns of St. Vith and Bastogne, which narrowed their attack front. By

Right: *In Holland, late 1944. "The Germans had blown up the dike between Arnhem and Nijmegen, resulting in the low lands being flooded. This complicated the evacuation as the dams were the only means to travel across the country. We were low on ammunition and transport vehicles. Furthermore, American aircraft and artillery took on isolated soldiers, which speaks volumes about the American way of waging war." (Unteroffizier Mayer, 21st Parachute Engineer Regiment)*

the 22nd, the Americans, having lost 8000 of 22,000 men at St. Vith, pulled back from the town, but the men of the 28th Infantry, 10th and 101st Airborne Divisions continued to hold out in Bastogne against one infantry and two panzer divisions. On the same day the Germans launched their last attempt to reach the Meuse.

Fallschirmjäger units saw extensive action in the Ardennes Offensive, especially the 3rd Parachute Division, part of the Fifteenth Army deployed to the north, and the 5th Parachute Division, part of the Seventh Army. Though the paras of these units fought in the infantry role, there was to be one last airborne operation. Student devised the operation, codename "Stosser", to support the offensive. He placed the mission under the command of Oberst von der Heydte, who was instructed to form a group of 1200 men drawn from the First Parachute Army and formed into four infantry companies, plus a heavy weapons company, and a signals and engineer platoon. Unfortunately, the various battalion commanders within the army had no wish to part with their best men, and so von der Heydte was sent mediocre troops at best. This would not augur well for the mission.

Above: *One of the most famous photographs of World War II: Fallschirmjäger hitch a ride on a Tiger II in the Ardennes. Both the 3rd and 5th Parachute Divisions took part in the offensive, both of them having been rebuilt after the losses suffered in France. Their effectiveness suffered accordingly. The 3rd, for example, had few experienced personnel left and its commander, Generalmajor Richard Schimpf, knew little about infantry tactics.*

Below: *Well-wrapped Fallschirmjäger in the Ardennes Offensive. The 5th Parachute Division was on the wing of the Seventh Panzer Army, and provided flank cover for the Fifth Panzer Army. The Seventh's commander, General Erich Brandenberger, was impressed by its performance during the offensive: "On 15 Dec 44, 5 FJ Div scored a particularly fine success. While the advance elements of the division pushed ahead to reach Harlange, the reinforced engineer battalion, which had turned off northward, was able to encircle a strong group. Several hundred prisoners were taken, with rich booty."*

His unit was under the command of the Sixth SS Panzer Army, and was ordered to drop on the main road junction 11km (6.87 miles) north of Malmédy — the main route for US reinforcements being sent to the area. The drop would be made at night, with no photographs of the area or prior reconnaissance provided. The drop was scheduled to be made at 04:30 hours on 16 December, but transport problems resulted in the paras getting to the airfields at Lippespringe and Padeborn late. Kampfgruppe (Battle Group) *Heydte* eventually boarded the aircraft and took off in appalling weather. Allied flak dispersed the formation and pilot error ensured that the Fallschirmjäger were dispersed over a wide area. In fact, on the ground von der Heydte could only assemble 125 men, and all the heavy weapons were lost.

By the 17th a further 150 men came in to him. It was pitiful, but the widely dispersed drops convinced the Allies that whole enemy airborne divisions had been dropped. They therefore diverted units to search for them instead of sending

them to the front. Von der Heydte, cut off, unable to make contact with the Sixth SS Panzer Army and receiving no supplies from the Luftwaffe, decided to form an assault group and break through Allied lines to reach safety. The attack failed, and so on 21 December he formed his command into two- and three-man groups to increase the likelihood of getting through enemy lines. However, many of his men were captured, and von der Heydte himself also fell into enemy hands. The last German airborne operation of World War II had ended in disaster.

On the ground, the 9th Parachute Regiment, part of the 3rd Parachute Division, fought its way to Lanzerath. Some paras were attached to Kampfgruppe *Peiper* (which was to achieve infamy in the Ardennes by massacring American

Above: *A para team in the Ardennes moves past a knocked-out US Sherman tank. The soldier second from right carries a Panzerschreck (Tank Terror). It appears to be a Model 54 as it has a shield to protect the firer from rocket exhaust. A fully trained two-man team could fire 4–5 88mm rockets in a minute. The soldier on the far left has a Panzerfaust (Tank Fist), a one-shot antitank weapon capable of penetrating up to 200mm (7.8in) of armour.*

Left: *A member of Kampfgruppe Heydte on the ground in the Ardennes. The last parachute assault of the Fallschirmjäger in World War II was a fiasco. The reasons were summed up succinctly in a report on German airborne operations compiled after the war, one of the contributors being von der Heydte himself: "The force committed was far too small (only one battalion took part in the attack); the training of parachute troops and troop-carrier squadrons was inadequate; the Allies had superiority in the air; the weather was unfavourable; preparations and instructions were deficient; the attack by ground forces miscarried. In short, almost every prerequisite of success was lacking."*

prisoners of war at Malmédy), while the rest of the regiment joined other SS units and had reached Schoppen by 19 December. Other elements of the 3rd Parachute Division had reached Ligneuville by 20 December, but increasing US pressure then halted their progress.

The 5th Parachute Division, protecting the southern flank of the Fifth Panzer Army as it advanced to the River Maas, ran into heavy US resistance almost immediately and had to rely on the assault guns of the 11th Self-Propelled Parachute Brigade to aid the advance. The paras took Wiltz on 20 December, along with 1000 prisoners, 25 Sherman tanks and a number of trucks. However, it was their last success. By the 23rd the division was being attacked by Allied aircraft, suffering from fuel shortages and assaulted by elements of the US Third Army and the US 4th Armored Division. It was pushed back to Bastogne, where the US 101st Airborne Division was still besieged by

Below: *German dead near Bastogne, which elements of the 5th Parachute Division assaulted on Christmas Eve 1944. Despite the courage and resilience of its personnel, the division suffered from a chronic lack of artillery and vehicles, and many of its men were low on ammunition and weapons.*

surrounding German units. The 5th took part in an abortive attack on the town on Christmas Eve, but afterwards, together with other units, was pushed back to the offensive's start line. "Watch on the Rhine" was over.

Collapse in the West

The last vestiges of the German "bulge" in the Ardennes was wiped out on 28 January 1945. The total cost to the Germans in manpower for their offensive was 100,000 killed, wounded and captured. The Americans lost 81,000 killed, wounded or captured, the British 1400. Both sides lost heavily in hardware: up to 800 tanks each. The Germans also lost up to 1000 aircraft. The Fallschirmjäger divisions were now shadows of their former selves, being depleted in both manpower and hardware. Nevertheless, their morale was still high and they continued fighting.

The 2nd Parachute Division was reformed in Holland in late 1944 and went into action in January 1945. It ended the war in the Ruhr Pocket in April 1945. The 3rd Parachute Division, having been mauled in the Battle of the Bulge, was decimated in the defensive battles in Germany in 1945. It too surrendered in the Ruhr Pocket, together with the 5th Parachute Division. The 1st Parachute Army continued its defence of Holland and the approaches to the Rhine into 1945, before being deployed to defend the east bank of the river. It surrendered in the Oldenburg area in April 1945.

In the last few weeks of the war parachute divisions in name only were raised, along with numerous battalions recruited from Luftwaffe training or ground units. They were thrown into action to shore up tattered defence lines or launch hopeless counterattacks. Invariably young, the members of such units fought with determination and courage against hopeless odds, and maintained

Below: *Fallschirmjäger give themselves up to US troops as the Third Reich collapses in April 1945. For nearly six years the airborne troops had fought valiantly, as Student himself remarked: "the German parachute troops have on every front exhibited the best soldierly virtues, great offensive spirit, and most of all an unsurpassed willingness to sacrifice."*

Above: *German prisoners taken in the Ruhr Pocket in April 1945, among them the remnants of the 2nd, 3rd and 5th Parachute Divisions.*

the Fallschirmjäger spirit to the end. The 11th Parachute Division was formed in March 1945 in the Linz area, though this unit was a division in name only. By 20 April only 4450 men had been collected. These personnel were committed to the battle in the West piecemeal, fighting on to the surrender of Germany in early May. The division was commanded by Oberst Walter Gericke. The 20th Parachute Division was apparently formed in northern Holland in March 1945, though its actions and fate are unknown. Even less is known about the 21st Parachute Division, which was formed in April 1945. By the end of April there was little fuel, ammunition or weapons left to equip these units, much less transport to get them to the battle areas. By 8 May all fighting in the West came to an end.

Above: *Fallschirmjäger salute the heavily laden Fieseler Storch aircraft about to take off from the Gran Sasso plateau with the rescued Il Duce on board.*

SPECIALIST ACTIONS

As well as large-scale missions, airborne forces could also be used for small, precision insertions that could be stunning successes. However, such missions carried a high risk, and the margin between success and failure was slim. As the Germans discovered to their cost, the price for audacity could be disaster and high casualties.

Left: *Otto Skorzeny, the SS officer who led the rescue of Mussolini from Gran Sasso in September 1943. Though the paratroopers used were Luftwaffe men, the SS and Skorzeny took the credit for the mission, with Skorzeny winning himself a Knight's Cross.*

During the war there were a number of small-scale Fallschirmjäger actions that characterise the spirit of Germany's airborne forces. The first, and most spectacular, was the rescue of the Italian dictator Benito Mussolini from Gran Sasso in Italy.

Successive Axis reverses in North Africa and Sicily had weakened the credibility of Mussolini's fascist regime, which he himself recognised. He met Adolf Hitler at Feltre in the Veneto on 17 July 1943 with the intention of announcing to the German Führer that Italy was withdrawing from the war. However, he was overawed by his fellow dictator and stayed silent. Events were now taken out of his hands: on 24 July the Italian Fascist Grand Council met and voted military powers to the king. The next day, after an interview with the king, Mussolini was arrested and Marshal Pietro Badoglio formed a government.

Upon hearing of Mussolini's fall, Hitler decided that Italy would not be allowed to withdraw from the war. His troops were in control of Rome and

north Italy, and they would be staying (see Chapter 7). As for *Il Duce*, the Führer decided that he should be rescued. He therefore summoned SS Captain Otto Skorzeny to his headquarters in East Prussia, declaring he would not "fail Italy's greatest son in his hour of need".

Though Skorzeny was in the Waffen-SS, for the purposes of the mission he was subordinated to the Luftwaffe. His immediate problem was to find Mussolini, which was solved when German radio intercepts pinpointed his whereabouts to the Gran Sasso plateau in the Apennines, 128km (80 miles) northeast of Rome. *Il Duce* was being held in a hotel on top of the plateau, which made his rescue a tricky problem. Skorzeny had three options: a ground assault, a parachute landing or a glider attack. A ground assault was ruled out because of the large number of troops required, and a parachute landing was impractical due to the very real possibility of the troops missing the plateau altogether. This left the glider option.

The operation is launched

On the afternoon of 12 September 1943, 12 fully manned DFS 230 gliders took off from the Practica de Mare airfield near Rome. On board were men drawn from the Waffen-SS and 7th Parachute Regiment (other paratroopers were despatched to capture the nearby airfield at Aquila), plus a pro-German Italian officer named General Spoleti who was taken to prevent unnecessary bloodshed. Four of the gliders were lost to Skorzeny during take-off and the flight, and as the remaining gliders approached their landing area behind the

Above: *A DFS 230 glider on the rocky slopes of Gran Sasso. The DFS 230 was a lightweight glider constructed of tubing and fabric which handled well in the air. Later models were fitted with a braking 'chute and even retro rockets in the nose. For take-off each glider had wheels which could be dropped during flight, which meant that landing was made on a ventral central skid. Occupants usually comprised a pilot and nine men. There was only one door, in the port rear, but "kick out" panels on either side of the fuselage could be removed for a quick escape. Over 2000 DFS 230s were manufactured in total.*

hotel he discovered it was totally unsuitable. In fact, it was a very steep hillside, and so the gliders had to land in front of the building. The aircraft made a crash landing in quick succession. Skorzeny sprinted towards the hotel, burst in and kicked the chair from beneath a wireless operator on the ground floor to prevent any communications with the outside world. The shocked Italian guards didn't fire a shot as the Waffen-SS and Fallschirmjäger troops secured the plateau and freed Mussolini. The only casualties were those troops in a glider that suffered a heavy crash landing.

Having rescued *Il Duce*, Skorzeny evacuated him and himself in a Fieseler Storch aircraft. The party travelled to Rome, then Vienna and on to East Prussia. For his part in the operation Skorzeny was awarded the Knight's Cross, while Mussolini exchanged one form of imprisonment for another.

Waffen-SS airborne units

As well as the Luftwaffe, the SS (Schutz Staffel) – Protection Squad – became involved in developing a parachute arm, and maintained a tiny organisation right up to the end of the war. The 500th SS-Fallschirmjäger Battalion was officially formulated on 6 September 1943, and was composed of personnel of the SS-Bewährungs Abteilung (SS Punishment Battalion). A penal unit, it was officered by volunteers from various Waffen-SS divisions, with half the "other ranks" being genuine volunteers. The other half were paroled prisoners from SS penal companies. These men were offered the chance to redeem their honour and clear their records by volunteering for service in the battalion and undertaking particularly dangerous missions. This newly formed unit was not held in high esteem, however, because of its high rate of personnel with questionable records. At this juncture, it is important to examine the implications of being "on penal detention".

Below: *Fallschirmjäger sprint into the attack at Gran Sasso. For the mission General Kurt Student gave Skorzeny the 1st Battalion of the 7th Parachute Regiment. It was a generous gesture, as the regiment had been formed in February 1943 in the Vannes/Bretagne area of France from XI Flieger Corps' Parachute Demonstration Battalion – an élite within an élite. The regiment's first commander was Oberst Ludwig Straub.*

SS-Oberführer Horst-Bender was a professional lawyer who spent his later career in legal posts with the Waffen-SS, SS Central Office and SS Legal Department. He ended the war as head of the legal detachment assigned to Himmler's personal staff and head of the Waffen-SS judge advocate's department, and was instrumental in the formulation of the policy that provided the powers to inaugurate the unit.

On 20 August 1942, Hitler gave Otto Thierack, who had been appointed Minister of Justice, a brief empowering him to deviate from any existing law to establish a National Socialist Administration of Justice. Josef Göbbels, Minister of Propaganda, suggested that in addition to Jews and gypsies, many more could be "exterminated by work". Martin Bormann, Nazi Party Minister, gave his approval for Thierack to see Himmler at Zhitomir. Here, in the presence of Bender and SS-Gruppenführer und Generalleutnant der Polizei und Waffen-SS Bruno Streckenbach, they reached an agreement on a principal entitled "the delivery of asocial elements to the Reichsführer-SS to be worked to death". The initial proposal was to be applied to all Jews and gypsies, to Poles imprisoned for three or more years, and to Czechs and Germans serving life sentences.

Himmler's meeting refined this to all Germans serving sentences of eight years and over and all persons already in "protective custody". Bender then made other recommendations on penal detention. Himmler regarded the Dirlewanger penal unit, another Waffen-SS formation, as an essential component of Waffen-SS discipline, linking it with the 500th SS-Fallschirmjäger Battalion as a way to redeem lost honour. Bender objected when, in March 1944, SS-Obergruppenführer Gottlob Berger wanted to transfer all the SS men in detention at Marienwerder to the Dirlewanger unit. Bender advised Himmler to send only those convicted of criminal offences who would not be accepted by the parachute unit.

Below: *The Campo Imperatore Hotel on Gran Sasso, where Mussolini was detained in September 1943. While he was there he learned of the Italian surrender and armistice, one of the conditions of which was that he was to be handed over to the Allies. However, the Germans had other ideas.*

Above: Il Duce *is free! The operation had been such a success that not a single shot was fired by either side during the rescue. The first words Skorzeny said to Mussolini were: "Duce! The Führer has sent me! You are free!" However, he soon realised that he was merely swapping one form of imprisonment for another, for now he had become a puppet of the German dictator.*

By early 1941, the planning for the German attack on the Soviet Union made it essential for Yugoslavia to be brought under Axis control and, as had happened so often before, the breakdown of diplomacy heralded a German onslaught (see Chapter 4). The whole operation was not so much a victory for German arms as for German staff planning and organisation. "Operation Punishment", as it was called, began on Palm Sunday: 6 April 1941. "Belgrade must be destroyed by continuous day and night air attacks", Hitler had decreed. He was to have his swift victory as the Wehrmacht achieved another easy triumph over an inferior enemy.

However, during the subsequent German occupation the Yugoslav partisan forces, the Jugoslav National Army of Liberation (JANL), grew in strength and numbers to such an extent that it seriously undermined the German military presence. Whole regions of the country had been recaptured, threatening the other German-occupied areas. German offensives using ground troops had had little military success. The tactics of the partisan forces were to avoid direct confrontation: when faced with a superior enemy force they simply dispersed and took refuge in the mountains. In the early months of the occupation these tactics had worked well. When the organisation of corps and divisions had been achieved and a National Headquarters established, however, such evasion was no longer a plausible strategy. The efforts to disperse, then reconstitute, National Headquarters not only consumed time and effort, but led to disruption of partisan operations.

The German offensive operations in 1942 and 1943 had given rise to several such moves by JANL Headquarters. A fifth offensive opened in the autumn of 1943, codenamed Operation "Fireball", and the inconvenience was again repeated. In this operation, the German 1st Mountain Division was deployed along with the Croatian 369th Division, elements of the 187th Division, and the 7th SS Freiwilligen-Gebirgs Division *Prinz Eugen*, part of V SS Mountain Corps. The Bulgarians contributed one division. Also included in the order of battle were detachments of a Brandenburg battalion who were specialists in intelligence and counterintelligence operations. The offensive was called off on 18 December, due to bad planning and after the Bulgarians had refused to carry out their orders (they were now desperate to extricate themselves from their disastrous alliance with Germany).

Tito – elusive foe

In 1944, in an attempt to keep up the pressure, the offensive was resumed under the codename "Snow Flurry", though without the Bulgarians or the 7th SS Freiwilligen-Gebirgs Division *Prinz Eugen*. These had been withdrawn for further training and regrouping in the Dubrovnik region. Himmler felt assured that he could count on his Moslem SS men to deal mercilessly with the Serbs, and so ordered in the 13th SS Waffen-Gebirgs Division *Handschar* to replace them. His trust was not misplaced. The division distinguished itself by the scale of the atrocities it committed in this, its first major action. Atrocities included SS men cutting out their victims' hearts to ensure that they were indeed dead. This offensive ground to a halt, as did all previous ones, without achieving much more than moving the enemy from one region to another. Josip Tito, leader of the partisans, divided his army into four, sending one corps to each quarter of the country. Thus no single offensive could hope to eliminate his movement.

"Snow Flurry" forced Tito to yet again relocate his headquarters, this time from Jajce to the small town of Drvar in the Bosnian highlands. Here, it was established in a cave situated in a narrow crack in the mountains that surrounded the town. The cave was not only concealed from the air, making it an almost impossible target to detect and hit, it also had an exit through which the partisan leader could make good his escape if enemy forces were about to trap him. By the spring of 1944, the German High Command decided that the only

Below: *To the right of Mussolini is General Spoleti, who had been asked to take part in the Gran Sasso operation to prevent unnecessary bloodshed. It was a ploy that worked, for when the gliders landed Spoleti raced towards the hotel shouting: "Don't shoot! Don't shoot!' And the Carabinieri guards didn't shoot.*

Above: *Oberleutnant von Berlepsch (right), commander of the 1st Company, 7th Parachute Regiment, shakes the hand of Major Mors, commander of the regiment's 1st Battalion. It was von Berlepsch's company that spearheaded the Gran Sasso operation. Note the DFS 230 glider in the top right-hand corner of the photograph.*

way to deal the partisans a mortal blow was to kill or capture their commander. To accomplish this they devised an audacious plan using an airborne assault. Since their costly victory at Crete in May 1941, the German parachute formations had been mainly employed as élite infantry rather than airborne troops. It was the SS, newcomers in this aspect of warfare, which was to provide the strike force for this projected operation, codenamed "Knight's Move". A particularly hazardous venture, the choice of date for the operation, which may have been deliberate, was 25 May 1944 – Tito's birthday.

The skies over Yugoslavia at this time were still owned by the Luftwaffe, thus suspected or known partisan strongholds could be strafed and bombed almost at will. To offset this undoubted tactical advantage, German airborne troops would go into battle with no heavy weapons and limited quantities of ammunition. The SS-Fallschirmjäger Battalion also had the handicaps of being outnumbered and fighting an enemy who was well equipped and armed. The SS airborne troops could also only rely on supplies dropped from the air, and the aircraft would have to fly through a corridor of flak to deliver the supplies.

All ranks of the 500th SS-Fallschirmjäger Battalion had been trained or given refresher training at the Kralyevo Parachute School in Serbia, and their first mission would be bloody and have a slim chance of success. It was just the sort of operation in which desperate men could redeem their lost honour, those who survived, that is. Under SS-Hauptsturmführer Rybka's leadership, the unit

was to be landed by parachute and glider onto a hillside plateau that afforded sufficient flat ground to allow for a glider landing. The location was the Bosnian industrial area of Drvar, the site of Marshal Tito's mountain headquarters. The aim of the operation was to capture the guerrilla leader and destroy his partisan movement. The 500th SS-Fallschirmjäger Battalion, numbering over 600 men, was to be landed in the centre of an area held by at least 12,000 partisans. Unfortunately, the paratroopers could not be transported in a single lift due to lack of aircraft. The initial drop would be made at 07:00 hours and the second, a reinforcement wave, would arrive at approximately midday. The paratroopers' initial task would be to seize and hold the ground. That accomplished, the gliderborne element, of which there were insufficient DFS 230 gliders available to make more than one assault, would land and capture the partisan commander. The battalion would then hold the area until relieved by a battle group of army and Waffen-SS units. The battle group was under orders to carry out the relief operation during the first day of the airborne drop.

The attack goes in

According to plan, just after 07:00 hours on 25 May, a flight of Junkers Ju 52 transport aircraft began to disgorge their cargo of paratroopers of SS-Hauptsturmführer Rybka's battalion over Drvar. The first wave had been divided into three detachments; Rybka dropped with the first group. These were followed by waves of glider-towing aircraft, numbering about 40 in all. Having flung themselves from their transport aircraft, the paratroopers landed and within minutes had captured the deserted town and its surrounding areas. With the landing area secured, the circling gliders descended and disembarked the 320-man assault detachment. This was subdivided into six groups, each

Above: *To the right of Mussolini strides Otto Skorzeny, dressed in the tropical uniform of a Luftwaffe captain. All the 26 members of Skorzeny's Waffen-SS detachment wore Luftwaffe uniforms. Skorzeny had been responsible for locating Mussolini, but later assumed all credit for his rescue.*

being assigned a special objective. The task of attacking the "Citadel", Tito's cave headquarters, fell to Panther, the largest glider group, which consisted of 110 men. It was to this unit that Rybka and his group of paratroopers were to attach themselves. They marched from the town towards the area on the hillside where Panther Group's six gliders had come to a halt. The attack undoubtedly took the defenders by surprise, but the Germans still ran into problems. Several gliders had crashed on landing, killing all their occupants. Fortunately, the pilots of the six gliders of Panther Group had each landed within yards of the objective: the mouth of the cave. Rybka's initial observation was that, seeing how close the gliders had landed to the target, he would be able to organise the men to mount a speedy assault that would result in the capture of Tito. The omens for success looked good.

The reaction of the guerrilla leader's escort battalion and other Yugoslav troops positioned around the cave entrance was prompt, though, and even as the flimsy wooden gliders skated across the rocky terrain they were riddled with gunfire. When Rybka arrived he found that the site had been turned into a slaughterhouse. He summoned the SS paratroopers in the town, firing a red flare that brought most of them to him at the double. Possessing heavy weapons and superior in numbers, the partisans had the advantage of holding ground extensively strengthened with field defences. To combat those fearful odds, the SS paratroopers were armed with nothing more than their personal courage, training and their unshakeable believe in the SS ethos. They rallied and mounted a concentrated effort to take the "Citadel", but it was to be an unequal battle.

Below: *These scruffy Fallschirmjäger were part of a detachment sent to secure the cable car station at the foot of Monte Corno during the Gran Sasso operation. Actually the cable car was inoperative, leading to the rescued Italian dictator being flown off the plateau in a Fieseler Storch flown by General Student's own pilot, Captain Gerlach. After take-off the aircraft dived down into the valley before Gerlach could pull it into level flight. Mussolini was flown to the Practica de Mare airfield, transferred to a Heinkel and then taken on to Vienna. From there he was taken to Munich and then on to Hitler's headquarters in East Prussia.*

Due to the defenders' superior firepower, the first assault collapsed. The SS group reformed, though, and throughout the morning attacked continuously, throwing wave upon wave against the enemy. Some attacks gained ground, while in others ground was lost. During the morning's furious encounters the SS never managed to enter Tito's cave. As midday approached it was obvious to all that "Knight's Move" had no chance of obtaining its objective.

Now heavily reinforced, the partisan units began to take the initiative and counterattacked. At midday, a second air drop of SS paratroopers took place, but by this time Allied air units at Bari in Italy had been alerted to what was going on and were now flying sorties over the battle zone. The arrival of the SS

Left: *Preparing for a mission in 1943 or 1944. The days of the large-scale airborne drops were over by this time, but the Fallschirmjäger still undertook a number of small drops. One example was the attack on the island of Elba on 17 September 1943. Following the Allied invasion of Italy in early September (see Chapter 7), the German High Command decided to secure Elba, which at the time was garrisoned by Italian troops. Following an aerial bombardment, men of the 3rd Battalion, 7th Parachute Regiment, landed on the island and rounded up the dazed garrison. The parachute drop was a complete success, but pointless as the Allies landed at Anzio – the occupation of Elba was not on their agenda.*

paratroopers' second wave brought little change to the now grave situation. The landing zone itself was swept by machine-gun and mortar fire, which meant the paratroopers suffered heavy losses. Yet another assault was made on the cave after the survivors had linked up with the main body of the battalion. This also failed. Fresh units were arriving on the Yugoslav side all the time, and were put into the line to relieve those who had borne the brunt of the first German attack.

Above: *Paratroopers pose with the new uniform of Marshal Tito after the Drvar operation in May 1944. As well as the Waffen-SS, the Brandenburgers were also involved in airborne operations. On 5 October 1943, for example, the Parachute Regiment of the Brandenburg Division seized the island of Kos in a gliderborne assault backed up by the 22nd Airlanding Division. Elements of the same units, reinforced by the 1st Battalion of the 2nd Parachute Regiment, also attacked the island of Leros on 12 November 1943 (the German High Command feared both islands would be used as a forward base for an invasion of the Balkans). Leros was heavily defended, and it took five days of fighting before the island was secure.*

The collapse of "Knight's Move"

The decision to withdraw from the cave area was taken reluctantly by Rybka late in the afternoon. The remnants of the battalion were to be concentrated inside the walls of the town cemetery until relieved. This, however, was not achieved until long after dark, by which time the SS paratroopers were exhausted. The 1st Mountain Division and the 7th SS Freiwilligen-Gebirgs Division *Prinz Eugen*, scheduled to link up with their airborne comrades within the first 24 hours, had failed to do so. Distances which appeared short on the battle maps at German Headquarters became much longer when every yard of the way was contested by partisan obstacles and ambushes.

Encircled by an enemy who was now supremely confident of being able to engage and annihilate them, at Drvar the men of the SS battalion held their breath. However, the Allies believed Tito's position to be so desperate that a decision was taken to airlift him out. On 3 June, therefore, an RAF Dakota flew him to Italy, and a week later he set up new headquarters on the British/partisan-held island of Vis.

At Drvar, the SS battalion had been weakened by the losses it had sustained in killed and wounded, but its morale was still high. During the ensuing cold,

dark night, each partisan attack was fought off valiantly. As dawn approached, in the distance could be heard a noise drawing closer: the ripping-sheet sound of MG 42s at work. Then, the throaty cough of engines was audible near the cemetery, heralding the approach of a group of Schwimmwagen vehicles. They carried a battle group from the 13th Regiment of the 7th SS Freiwilligen-Gebirgs Division *Prinz Eugen*, which had penetrated partisan lines. The short but disastrous battle was over. The outcome of operation "Knight's Moves" was that the partisans had suffered approximately 6000 casualties. On the other hand, when the battalion roll call was held after the fighting was over only 200 men responded to their names. The rest were dead or wounded. The Germans had failed in their main objective of capturing Tito. However, as a consolation prize, they had relived him of his new debonair Marshal of Yugoslavia uniform!

Due to the excellent fighting ability displayed in the Drvar operation, Himmler, delighted by its courage and steadfastness, especially when surrounded in the cemetery, restored the ranks and insignia of the men with questionable records. The unit was retitled to become the 600th SS-Fallschirmjäger Battalion. Not only did this new title sever any connection with Battalion 500, but it also eliminated confusion with the SS-Jäger Battalion (SS Rifle Battalion) 500. On 10 November 1944, the 600th SS-Fallschirmjäger Battalion became part of the SS-Jagdverbande (SS Hunting Units — used for anti-partisan operations and the like). It did retain its identity, however, and continued to operate as a separate unit. Within the SS-Jagdverbande, sub-units existed such as SS-Sturmbataillon (SS Assault Battalion) 500, which had two parachute-trained companies attached to it: Dora I and Dora II. The 600th SS-Fallschirmjäger Battalion continued to serve as a combat unit on the Eastern Front until the end of the war. Needless to say, it suffered heavy casualties as the German armed forces tried to stem the advance of the Red Army.

Above: *Otto Skorzeny photographed in Budapest. The entrance to the building is guarded by two Waffen-SS paratroopers. The 600th SS-Fallschirmjäger Battalion was used as a "fire brigade" on the Eastern Front in the latter stages of the war, fighting up until April 1945 on the Oder Front. Its survivors managed to surrender to US forces and therefore avoided falling into Soviet hands and almost certain execution.*

7TH FLIEGER DIVISION ORDER OF BATTLE, NOVEMBER 1938

Divisional headquarters (Tempelhof)
Major-General Student

1st Battalion, 1st Parachute Regiment (Stendal)
Oberstleutnant Bräuer

Parachute Infantry Battalion (Braunschweig)
Major Heidrich

Airlanding Battalion
Major Sydow

***General Göring* Regiment (Berlin)**
Composed of:
Infantry Gun Company (Gardelegen)
1st Lieutenant Schram

Medical Company (Gardelegen)
Major Dieringshofen

Glider Detachment (Prenzlau)
Lieutenant Kiess

Signals Company (Berlin)
1st Lieutenant Schleicher

Training School (Stendal)
Major Reinberger

1st and 2nd Air Transport Groups
Captain Morzik

At the beginning of 1939, there was a complete reorganisation of Germany's airborne detachments. The loose framework that had hitherto sufficed needed to be replaced by a more formal establishment if the 7th Flieger Division was to become a division in the full sense of that term. The establishment of a standard German infantry division was three rifle regiments, each of three battalions. The 7th Flieger Division had, at the beginning of 1939, only one parachute rifle regiment with one battalion. Though divisional strength included Heidrich's Parachute Infantry Battalion and Sydow's Airlanding Battalion of the *General Göring* Regiment, these had not been formally established as part of the parachute regiment. When that amalgamation was carried out, Heidrich's unit became the 2nd Parachute Battalion and Sydow's unit the 3rd Parachute Battalion of the 1st Parachute Regiment respectively. A headquarters was established, and Bräuer assumed command of the 1st Parachute Regiment. He was succeeded in the post of commander of the 1st Battalion by Major von Grazy. With the formal establishment of the first of the division's three regiments at last completed, in June 1939 work commenced on forming the 2nd Parachute Regiment. By the end of July, two battalions had been raised for this unit.

1944 PARACHUTE DIVISION ORDER OF BATTLE

The maximum strength of the division was 15,976 men. It was composed of three parachute regiments, an antitank battalion, headquarters and supporting units.

Parachute Regiment (3206 men)
Composed of:
Three battalions, plus
one antitank company (186 men) with
three towed 75mm anti-tank guns
one mortar company (163 men) with
9–12 120mm mortars

Parachute Battalion (853 men)
Composed of:
three rifle companies (170 men each)
one machine-gun company (205 men)
with eight heavy machine guns
four 81mm mortars
two 75mm light recoilless guns

Artillery Regiment (1571 men)
Composed of:
one battalion of three batteries with
12 75mm mountain guns
one battalion of three batteries with
12 105mm recoilless guns

Mortar Battalion (594 men)
Composed of:
three mortar companies (each one
equipped with 12 120mm mortars)

Antitank Battalion (484 men)
Composed of:
one company with
12 towed 75mm antitank guns
one company with
14 75mm self-propelled guns
one antiaircraft company with
12 20mm self-propelled antiaircraft guns

Pioneer Battalion (620 men)
Composed of:
three pioneer companies
one machine-gun company

Antiaircraft Battalion (824 men)
Composed of:
two heavy antiaircraft batteries (each one
equipped with six 88mm guns)
one light antiaircraft company with
18 towed 20mm antiaircraft guns

Signals Battalion (379 men)
Composed of:
one radio company
one telephone company
one light signals company

Medical Battalion (800 men)
Composed of:
two medical companies
one field hospital
one light medical company

Reconnaissance Company (200 men)

FALLSCHIRMJÄGER KNIGHT'S CROSS HOLDERS

NAME	RANK	DATE OF AWARD	NAME	RANK	DATE OF AWARD
Abratis, Herbert	Hauptmann	24.10.44	Genz, Alfred	Oberleutnant	14.6.41
Adolff, Paul	Major	26.3.43	*Gericke, Walter	Hauptmann	14.6.41
Altmann, Gustav	Oberleutnant	12.5.40	Germer, Ernst	Feldwebel	29.10.44
Arpke, Helmut	Feldwebel	13.5.40	Gersteuer, Günther	Major	28.4.45
von Baer, Bern (HG)	Oberstleutnant	13.1.44	Gerstner, Siegfried	Major	13.9.44
Barmetler, Josef	Oberleutnant	9.7.41	Görtz, Hellmulth	Feldwebel	24.5.40
Becker, Karl-Heinz	Oberleutnant	9.7.41	Graf, Rudolf (HG)	Oberleutnant	6.10.41
Behre, Freidrich (HG)	Leutnant	9.5.45	*Grassmel, Franz	Maj.d.R.	8.4.44
Beine, Erich	Hauptmann	5.9.44	*Gröschke, Kurt	Major	9.6.44
Bellinger, Hans-Josif (HG)	Hauptmann	30.9.44	Grünewald, Georg	Oberfeldwebel	29.10.44
Berger, Karl	Leutnant	7.2.45	Grunhold, Werner (HG)	Unteroffizier	30.11.44
Berneike, Rudolf	Major	15.3.45	Hagl, Andreas	Oberleutnant	9.7.41
Bertram, Karl-Eric	Oberstleutnant	16.3.45	Hahm, Konstantin (HG)	Major	9.6.44
Beyer, Herbert	Hauptmann	9.6.44	Hamer, Reins	Hauptmann	5.9.44
Birnbaum, Fritz (HG)	Oberfeldwebel	19.10.44	Hansen, Hans-Christian (HG)	Hauptmann	11.2.45
Blauensteiner, Ernst	Oberstleutnant	29.10.44	Hartelt, Wolfgang (HG)	Oberfeldwebel	23.2.45
Blücher, Wolfgang	Lt.d.R.	24.5.40	Hauber, Freidrich	Hauptmann	5.9.44
Boehlein, Rudolf	Oberleutnant	30.11.44	*Heidrich, Richard	Oberst	14.6.41
Böhmler, Rudolf	Major	26.3.44	*Heilmann, Ludwig	Major	14.6.41
Bräuer, Bruno	Oberst	24.5.40	Hellmann Erich	Leutnant	6.10.44
Briegel, Hans (HG)	Major	17.1.45	Hengstler, Richard	Hauptmann	28.4.45
Büttner, Manfred	Feldwebel	29.4.45	Herbet, Erhard (HG)	Oberfeldwebel	26.3.45
*Conrath, Paul (HG)	Oberst	4.9.41	Herrmann, Harry	Oberleutnant	9.7.41
le Coutre, Georg	Leutnant	7.2.45	Herzbach, Max	Hauptmann	13.9.44
Delica, Egon	Leutnant	12.5.40	von Heydebreck, Georg (HG)	Oberst	25.6.44
Deutsch, Heinz	Lt.d.R.	28.4.45	*von der Heydte, Freiherr	Hauptmann	9.7.41
Donth, Rudolf	Feldwebel	14.1.45	Hoefeld, Robert	Oberleutnant	18.5.43
*Egger, Reinhard	Oberleutnant	9.7.41	Hübner, Edward	Hauptmann	9.5.45
Engelhardt, Johann	Oberleutnant	29.2.44	Itzen, Dirk (HG)	Leutnant	23.11.41
Erdmann, Wolfgang	Generalleutnant	8.2.45	Jacob, Georg-Rupert	Oberleutnant	13.9.44
Ewald, Werner	Major	12.9.44	Jäger, Rudolf	Ob.Asst.	13.5.40
Fitz, Josef-August (HG)	Hauptmann	11.12.42	Jamrowski, Siegfried	Oberleutnant	9.6.44
Foltin, Ferdinand	Hauptmann	9.6.44	Jungwirth, Hans	Major	9.5.45
Francois, Edmund (HG)	Hauptmann	20.10.44	Kalow, Siegfried (HG)	Unteroffizier	29.10.44
Fries, Herbert	Gefreiter	5.9.44	Kempke, Wilhelm	Feldwebel	21.8.41
Frömming, Ernst	Major	18.11.44	Kerfin, Horst	Oberleutnant	24.5.40
Fulda, Wilhelm	Leutnant	14.6.41	Kerutt, Hellmut	Major	2.2.45
Gast, Robert	Leutnant	6.10.44	Kiefer, Edward (HG)	Hauptmann	18.5.43

Witzig, Rudolf

Beyer, Herbert

Germer, Ernst

Kurz, Rudolf

Görtz, Helmuth

Schuster, Erich

Reininghaus, Adolf

Delica, Egon

NAME	RANK	DATE OF AWARD	NAME	RANK	DATE OF AWARD
Kiess, Walter	Oberleutnant	12.5.40	Pade, Gerhard	Major	30.4.45
Klein, Armin (HG)	Leutnant	12.3.45	Paul, Hugo	Hauptmann	18.11.44
Kluge, Walter (HG)	Major	2.8.43	Peitsch, Herbert	Gefreiter	29.10.44
Knaf, Walter (HG)	Leutnant	4.4.44	*Pietzonka, Erich	Oberstleutnant	5.9.44
Koch, Karl	Oberfeldwebel	27.10.44	Prager, Fritz	Hauptmann	24.5.40
Koch, Walter	Hauptmann	10.5.40	Plapper, Albert (HG)	Gefreiter	30.11.44
Koch, Willi	Oberfeldwebel	9.6.44	Quednow, Fritz (HG)	Hauptmann	5.4.44
Koenig, Heinz (HG)	Leutnant	8.2.45	Rademacher, Emil (HG)	Gefreiter	23.2.45
Köppen, Eckardt (HG)	Feldwebel	15.3.45	*Ramcke, Harmann-Bernhard	Oberst	21.8.41
Koepsell, Herbert (HG)	Unteroffizier	7.2.45	Rammelt, Siegfried	Leutnant	9.6.44
Kratzert, Rudolf	Hauptmann	9.6.44	Rapräger, Ernst-Wilhelm	Oberleutnant	10.5.43
Kraus, Rupert (HG)	Oberleutnant	30.11.44	Rebholz, Robert (HG)	Hauptmann	2.8.43
Krink, Heinz	Leutnant	9.6.44	Reininghaus, Adolf	Oberfeldwebel	13.9.44
*Kroh, Hans	Major	21.8.41	Renisch, Paul-Ernst	Hauptmann	27.11.44
Kroymans, Willi	Oberleutnant	20.1.45	*Rennecke, Rudolf	Hauptmann	9.6.44
Kühne, Martin	Hauptmann	29.2.45	Renz, Joaihim (HG)	Hauptmann	6.12.44
Kuhlwilm, Wilhelm (HG)	Oberleutnant	30.11.44	Richter, Heinz	Leutnant	24.3.45
Kulp, Karl (HG)	Feldwebel	5.9.44	Ringler, Helmut	Leutnant	15.5.40
Kunkel, Kurt-Ernst	Leutnant	30.4.45	von Roon, Arnold	Oberleutnant	9.7.41
Kurz, Rudolf	Oberfeldwebel	18.11.44	*Rossmann, Karl (HG)	Oberleutnant	12.11.41
Langemeyer, Carl	St.Arzt.	18.11.44	Sander, Walter	Leutnant	28.2.45
Lehmann, Hans-Georg (HG)	Oberleutnant	10.10.44	Sandrock, Hans (HG)	Major	18.10.44
Leitenberger, Helmut (HG)	Leutnant	17.4.45	Sassen, Bruno	Feldwebel	22.2.42
Lepkowski, Erich	Leutnant	8.8.44	Schacht, Gerhard	Leutnant	12.5.40
Liebing, Walter	Major	2.2.45	Schächter, Martin	Leutnant	12.5.40
Lipp, Hans-Hermann	Hauptmann	31.10.44	Schäfer, Heinrich	Oberfeldwebel	8.8.44
Mager, Rolf	Hauptmann	31.10.44	Scheid, Johannes (HG)	Oberfeldwebel	21.6.43
Marscholek, Hans	Oberleutnant	31.10.44	Schimpf, Richard	Generalleutnant	6.10.44
*Meindl, Eugen	Generalmajor	14.6.41	Schimpke, Horst	Leutnant	5.9.44
*Meissner, Joachim	Leutnant	12.5.40	*Schirmer, Gerhart	Hauptmann	14.6.41
Menges, Otto	Oberfeldwebel	9.6.44	Schlemm, Alfred	Gl.Fj.Tz.	11.6.44
Mertins, Gerhard	Hauptmann	6.12.44	*Schmalz, Wilhelm (HG)	Major	28.11.40
Meyer, Elimar	Leutnant	17.9.43	Schmidt, Herbert	Oberleutnant	24.5.40
*Meyer, Heinz	Hauptmann	8.4.44	Schmidt, Leonhard	Hauptmann	30.4.45
Meyer-Schewe, Fredrich(HG)	Oberst	9.5.45	Schmidt, Werner	Major	5.4.44
Milch, Werner	Hauptmann	9.1.45	Schreiber, Kurt (HG)	Hauptmann	21.6.43
Mischke, Gerd	Leutnant	18.5.43	von der Schulenburg, Wolf-Werner	Major	20.6.43
von Necker, Hanns-Horst (HG)	Oberst	24.6.44	*Schulz, Karl-Lothar	Hauptmann	24.5.40
Neuhoff, Karl	Oberfeldwebel	9.6.44	Schuster, Erich	Feldwebel	21.8.41
Neumann, Heinrich	Ost. Asst.	21.8.41	Schwarzmann, Alfred	Oberleutnant	24.5.40
Orth, Heinrich	Oberfeldwebel	18.3.42			

Donth, Rudolf

Kempke, Wilhelm

Sassen, Bruno

Scheid, Johannes

Berger, Karl

Schäfer, Heinrich

Koch, Walter

Altmann, Gustav

NAME	RANK	DATE OF AWARD
Schweim, Heinz-Herbert (HG)	Major	28.2.45
Sempert, Günther	Hauptmann	30.9.44
Sniers, Hubert	Leutnant	24.10.44
Stecken, Albert	Major	28.4.45
Steets, Konrad (HG)	Gefreiter	30.11.44
Stehle, Werner	Leutnant	28.4.45
Stentzler, Edgar	Major	9.7.41
Stephani, Kurt	Major	30.9.44
Straehler-Pohl, Günther	Hauptmann	10.5.43
Stuchlik, Werner (HG)	Hauptmann	30.11.44
Stronk Wolfrann (HG)	Hauptmann	18.10.44
*Student, Kurt	Generalleutnant	12.5.40
Sturm, Alfred	Oberst	9.7.41
Tannert, Karl	Hauptmann	5.4.44
Teusen, Hans	Leutnant	14.6.41
Tietjen, Cord	Leutnant	27.5.40
Timm, Erich	Major	3.10.44
Toschka, Rudolf	Oberleutnant	14.6.41
Trebes, Horst	Oberleutnant	9.7.41
*Trettner, Heinrich	Major I.G.	24.5.40
Trotz, Herbert	Hauptmann	30.4.45
Tschierschwitz, Gerhard (HG)	Oberleutnant	6.12.44
Uhlig, Alexander	Oberfeldwebel	29.10.44
Veth, Kurt	Hauptmann	30.9.44
Vitali, Viktor	Leutnant	30.4.45
Wagner, Helmut	Leutnant	27.1.42
Wallhäuser, Heinz (HG)	Oberleutnant	30.11.44
Wangerin, Friedrich-Wilhelm	Hauptmann	24.10.44
Weck, Hans-Joachim	Leutnant	30.4.45
Welskop, Heinrich	Oberfeldwebel	20.8.41
Werner, Walter	Feldwebel	9.6.44
Wimmer, Johann (HG)	Hauptmann	28.1.45
Witte, Heinrich (HG)	Obergefreiter	18.5.43
Wittig, Hans-Karl	Feldwebel	5.2.44
Witzig, Rudolf	Oberleutnant	10.5.40
Zahn, Hilmar	Oberleutnant	9.6.44
Zierach, Otto	Oberleutnant	15.5.40

NAME	RANK	AWARD	DATE	AWARD NUMBER
Conrath, Paul	Glmj	Oakleaves	21.2.43	276
Egger, Reinhard	Oblt	Oakleaves	24.6.44	510
Fitz, Josef	Major	Oakleaves	24.6.44	511
Gericke, Walter	Major	Oakleaves	17.9.44	585
Grassmel, Franz	Major	Oakleaves	8.5.45	868
Gröschke, Kurt	Oblt	Oakleaves	9.1.45	643
Heidrich, Richard	Gllt	Oakleaves	5.2.44	382
		Swords	25.3.44	55
Heilmann, Ludwig	Oberst	Oakleaves	2.3.44	412
		Swords	15.5.44	67
von der Heydte Fr	Oblt	Oakleaves	18.10.44	617
Kroh, Hans	Oblt	Oakleaves	6.7.44	443
	Oberst	Swords	12.9.44	96
Meindl, Eugen	Gl Fs Tr	Oakleaves	31.8.44	564
		Swords	8.5.45	155
Meyer, Heinz	Hptm	Oakleaves	18.11.44	654
Pietzonka, Erich	Oberst	Oakleaves	16.9.44	584
Ramcke, Hermann	Glmj	Oakleaves	13.11.42	145
	Gllt	Swords	19.9.44	99
	Gllt	Swords & Diamonds	19.9.44	20
Rennecke, Rudolf	Major	Oakleaves	25.11.44	664
Rossmann, Karl	Major	Oakleaves	1.2.45	725
Schirmer, Gerhart	Oblt	Oakleaves	18.11.44	657
Schmalz, Wilhelm	Oberst	Oakleaves	23.12.43	358
Schulz, Karl-Lothar	Oberst	Oakleaves	20.4.44	459
		Swords	18.11.44	112
Student, Kurt	General	Oakleaves	27.9.43	305
Trettner, Heinrich	Glmj	Oakleaves	17.9.44	586
Witzig, Rudolf	Major	Oakleaves	25.11.44	662

Gl Fs Tr = General der Fallschirmtruppe

Gllt = Generalleutnant

Glmj = Generalmajor

Oblt = Oberstleutnant

* = Oakleaves, Swords or Swords and Diamonds winners

(HG) = *Hermann Göring* Division

Blauensteiner, Ernst *Becker, Karl-Heinz* *Barmetler, Josef* *Köppen, Eckardt* *Dr. Neumann* *Fries, Herbert* *Beine, Erich* *Bausch, Friedrich-Karl* *Abratis, Herbert*

INDEX

Numbers in *italics* refer to illustrations.